LOOKING FOR A FIGHT

LOOKING FOR A FIGHT

A Memoir

L Y N N   S N O W D E N   P I C K E T

THE DIAL PRESS

Published by
The Dial Press
Random House, Inc.
1540 Broadway
New York, New York 10036

This is a true story. Although most of the names that appear in this
book are real, in some instances names have been changed to
protect the privacy of those individuals.

The Dial Press® is a registered trademark of Random House, Inc., and the colophon
is a trademark of Random House, Inc.

Library of Congress Cataloging-in-Publication Data
Picket, Lynn Snowden
Looking for a fight : a memoir / Lynn Snowden Picket.
p.   cm.
ISBN 0-385-31584-8
1. Picket, Lynn Snowden.   2. Women boxers—United States—Biography.
I. Title.
GV1132.P53   A3   2000
796.83'092—dc21
00-063879

BOOK DESIGN BY GLEN M. EDELSTEIN

Manufactured in the United States of America
Published simultaneously in Canada

November 2000

10   9   8   7   6   5   4   3   2   1
BVG

To Bronson

CONTENTS

CONTENTS

It is not possible to fight beyond your strength,
even if you strive.
—HOMER

Grass grows, birds fly, waves pound the sand.
I just beat people up.
—MUHAMMAD ALI

GLEASON'S

THERE'S A GRITTY smell of old cement in Gleason's gym, of stained leather and ancient vinyl, the greasy reek of the small on-site snack bar and the ordered-in meals of rice and beans—the staple, I would later learn, of a trainer's diet. I can detect sweat, old sneakers, and the oily tang of metal weights, of gym bags that are never emptied or aired, of mildew and something else, something that I came to understand was the adrenaline scent of fear. Fear postponed, fear arriving, fear diverted.

Then there's the noise: the thudding of fists on vinyl, the

1

staccato beat of punching bags, the thwacking of jump ropes, the bellowing and barking of fighters and trainers, and the brutish finality of gloves landing hard on skin. Suddenly, there is a short, nearly cheerful-sounding *bzzzz*, a sound much like the front-door buzzer in a prewar building. This signals the two-and-a-half-minute mark in a three-minute round, the time for a final, heroic burst of effort. The noise level reaches a new crescendo until the sound of a prolonged flat alarm. The signal of a thirty-second break. Without the noise of physical exertion, the instruction, the yelling, the exhorting, a chorus of voices in English and Spanish suddenly bursts forth like a previously overpowered section in an orchestra.

Trainers mop foreheads, dispense water, reprimands, and advice until the flat buzzer sounds again. This is the start of a new round. It is a routine as predictable and time-driven as any factory work floor.

Gleason's consists of one very large room and at its center are four rings—three for boxing, one for wrestling. The heavy bags are hung in a large square near the main office. The paint is peeling off in flaky patches on the walls, and a few boxing posters (Sly Stallone as Rocky) break the monotony of neglect. The concrete floor is painted in spots and, in others, covered with shabby remnants of low-pile carpeting. There is no elevator, no handicapped access, no climate control, no classes, and no locker-room attendants.

The minute it takes me to cross the room toward my new trainer's office is enough to attract the attention of everyone in the place. At least twenty men are here working out, and about seven trainers and their assistants are milling around, plus assorted friends. Parked on some of the benches against the wall are old men who like to live vicariously through thick brutish bodies, and young toughs with no place else to hang out; both camps sometimes shout advice to boxers in the ring closest to them. I had just successfully completed the New York Marathon, but here, at Gleason's, I'm not a fellow athlete, I'm a visitor. Or worse, a girl.

In the fourth ring, the one for wrestling, two men are working on their routines. Theirs is not Olympic Greco-Roman–style combat, but the "professional" kind seen on television: blue-haired, leotard-wearing competitors with lightning bolts painted on their faces. In this ring, the ropes will stretch for slingshot antics, and the corners are padded. Until I went to Gleason's, I didn't realize professional wrestlers practiced their pratfalls. These men have a beer-brawler's build, broad and stocky, but no muscular definition. They ignore the bells and rest between falls, going at each other with a kind of impersonal, resigned determination, like football players in a practice scrimmage. They are, without question, the loudest individuals in the room, and the most completely ignored by all present. Wrestlers are boxing's ugly stepchildren.

I arrived at this place because I was looking for a fight— though I didn't know it at the time. I came into Gleason's the week before to buy boxing gear. My trainer, Mark Tenore, was not a serious boxing coach, so he knew that once I saw the gym, I would immediately crave its authenticity and would dare myself to come back.

Gleason's may be the most famous boxing gym in the world. Founded in 1937, it was originally located in the Bronx but moved to its present location on the Brooklyn waterfront in 1984. Every great boxer has passed through its doors, from Jake LaMotta and Muhammad Ali to more recent champions such as Junior Jones, Lonnie Bradley, and Riddick Bowe. The grimy, no-frills, blood-and-guts appeal is further enhanced by its low membership dues; aspiring boxers looking to fight their way out of poverty train beside champions and also, perhaps, the occasional lawyer or doctor looking for a workout beyond the confines of a health club.

Bruce Silverglade owns Gleason's. He is remarkably soft-spoken, of medium height and build, with dark curly hair that is beginning to recede. Mark and I were in his office buying the equipment when the talk turned to trainers. By this time I'd decided that Gleason's was for me, and Bruce knew it. Bruce doesn't look like a boxer, or a manager, or a gym owner, but more like an accountant who's stopped in to look at the books. His office, located off the gym floor, is a large spare room with two nearly empty steel desks, a few metal chairs, and two dingy beige touch-tone telephones.

Two young Hispanic guys seated by the wall were

watching our every move with interest. Their legs were splayed outward, and they were leaning over like benched basketball players watching a game. They had the lanky bodies of boys in adolescence that baggy clothes can't quite disguise. A couple of filthy windows looked down onto a narrow side street, and all available wall space was covered with fight posters and framed, autographed photos of boxers who'd passed through these doors. There was also a giant blowup of the famous *Esquire* magazine cover of Muhammad Ali glowering down at Sonny Liston, his face twisted in victorious triumph and macho rage.

Bruce asked me about what I wanted in a trainer, and I told him I imagined working with someone who dealt with "real boxers, professionals," not white-collar dilettantes. As someone who makes a living as a participatory journalist, I wanted the real deal at all times. I became a stripper to write a story about a strip club, I toured with a heavy-metal band as a roadie, I spent three days and nights on an aircraft carrier and a month with two police officers on their beat in Greenwich Village, all in the name of a story.

Enter Hector Roca: a heavyset Hispanic man with a face like a brick wall. He strode in, wearing a navy blue sweat suit with pristine white sneakers, and a large, thick gold rope chain around his neck. Bruce introduced us. Reaching to shake his hand, I instinctively braced myself for a crushing grip, but in fact his grip was gentle, tentative. I looked him directly in the eye, exactly the way he looked at me, and tried, without success, not to feel intimidated.

"I'm very tough," Hector said without smiling. His voice was rough, with a heavy accent. I nodded solemnly. I had my coat opened, so he could see I was in good shape; I was wearing a tight black turtleneck, black stretch pants, and boots. He'd taken this in already, as had the two kids by the wall, who'd been assessing my body for some time now. They looked at me in the same way that I've seen bettors at the track assess a horse.

"Don' go cryin' because I'm tough," said Hector.

"Don't worry about me," I said. He glanced at Mark, who looked at his feet.

"Les go talk. Leave you bodyguar' here," he said with a chuckle. I followed him back out into the hubbub of the gym proper, to his office, the second one down from Bruce's. The door, which was ajar, had a few fight posters on it, plus a paper sign with HECTOR ROCA handwritten in labored Gothic lettering.

"That was Mark. He's a trainer at my gym," I told him on the short walk. I didn't want him thinking that Mark is someone who might "cause trouble" here if someone punched me. I wanted to establish that I'm not a woman who lets a man fight all her battles.

A very young-looking Hispanic man with a baby face and velvety, hairless skin was on his way out of Hector's office. We were introduced. Hector looked at the young man in satin shorts with a mixture of awe and pride. I didn't catch his name, but the kid had the smug assurance of the lower-tier professional athlete who is convinced that every-one knows who he is.

"Maybe I have you spar with heem," said Hector. The kid laughed at the outrageousness of this suggestion. He was a little shorter than I am, so I extended my arm.

"My reach is longer than yours," I said to him, as if my reach were going to help against this wiry guy who could take me apart in less than twenty seconds. I sounded like an arrogant jerk, but it felt like the only fitting retort after he'd laughed at the thought of fighting a woman.

I wouldn't have that reaction today, but back then my bravado was part naïveté and part rage. Stunned by the recent dissolution of my marriage, and angry with my ex-husband, I was infuriated to find myself suddenly alone. Worse than that was the knowledge that I was now being perceived by my family and friends as vulnerable, help-less, and victimized, someone to be pitied and worried over. My mother, whom I adore, is nonetheless a chronic worrier. She would call me every day and I would be com-pelled to calm her fears about the future and ignore my own. And though my father said all the right things, I could tell he was thinking he'd have to now step in and take care of me. The fact that I'd supported myself since college seemed to be irrelevant. Single friends would grab my hand and ask if I was okay—as if I'd contracted a terminal illness. Married friends asked for details to reassure them-selves they weren't headed down the same path. "Maybe if you'd had kids . . ." ventured my friend Susan, as if that would have provided a distraction from the far deeper problems of my marriage.

The kid shook his head, smiled, and swaggered away. This was the first indication that the verbal sparring that had become second nature to me wasn't going to work worth a damn in this place.

I should have been alarmed, not only at my defensive reaction to that kid but at the canvas I had, in my bull-headedness, unwittingly stepped into—but I never could back down from a challenge. Friends and family had long since realized that a sure way to get me to do something I didn't want to do, or was afraid to do, was to accuse me of being scared to do it. As someone whose identity hinged on appearing to be brave, I was prone to remark that the worst thing a person could be was a coward. Foolish enough to believe my own hype, I absolutely thought I could climb into a boxing ring with real boxers and prevail simply because I had courage on my side.

Hector's office is about the size of a horse stall in an undersized barn. His desk faces the door, and he squeezed in behind it. A dirty window silhouetted his head. I took the only other option, the sturdy metal chair. There are some locked metal cabinets, a TV set and VCR, and lots of framed and signed photographs of boxers. By way of a ré-sumé, Hector told me some of the famous people he's trained. "Wesley Snipes. Harry Connick . . . the singer. Brad Davis. The one who died," he said mournfully. His thick accent made it difficult for me to follow his side of the conversation, but we managed. He mentioned he had trained one other woman. "She like women. A dyke," he said, chuckling like a boy enjoying a private joke in church. "She so good," he said, shaking his head, composing himself. "She fell in love with a girl and move to Paris." He looked at me, and I saw that I was expected to reassure him that I won't do the same.

"I don't have a boyfriend," I said, slightly mortified to be telling the truth. The few men I'd dated in the past several months had been spooked by my odd, controlling paranoia. I might spend the night with a man but would never let one into my apartment. So sacred had my private sanctum become, the small world I could control completely, that one man I dated never even learned my address. During my marriage, I was helpless against the various betrayals of my ex-husband, but now I felt safe knowing that I controlled absolutely everything within three rooms in New York City, that within those walls there would be no surprises, no variables. The woman sitting in Hector's office was fueled by a volatile mixture of anger, defiance, and incredible pain.

"I'm serious about this," I told him, anxious that he see me as a boxer, not as part of a couple, not as a woman. "I trained for the New York Marathon really hard, I just ran it a month ago, and I'm used to hard work." He looked at me suspiciously. "I don't go out partying at night," I added.

He nodded and told me I had to come in three times a

week minimum or I'd forget what I'd learned. Each lesson was ten dollars. I couldn't bring myself to say that I wasn't in good enough shape to start immediately, that I hadn't quite recovered from the physical toll of the Marathon: he might have thought I was just scared. I found myself agreeing to take my first lesson on Monday afternoon, the following week.

And so it began.

THE RING

DUCK UNDER THE ropes of a boxing ring, and the first thing you'll see is blood. There are bloodstains everywhere on the cream-colored canvas; old bloodstains appear as rusty brown patches; the new ones are bright red. There are speckles and blobs, smears and drips, in colors that range from deep brown to watery vermilion. My first thought is that I am looking at coffee stains, but then my mind shakes loose, and my stomach does a slow, nervous flip. It occurs to me that signing up for boxing lessons is not like signing up for an advanced aerobics class. People bleed in here.

Hector is standing below and waves his hands in a circular motion. "Move aroun'." Years of watching boxing on television and in the movies has made this moment seem strangely familiar. Still, I feel like I'm standing on a stage.

There's a weird give to the canvas, like the give in a supportive mattress. In parts of the ring, you sense that the boards underneath the surface are loose, or there's the equivalent of a tiny dip in the road or some small pothole, where your foot sinks deeper than it should. I tread carefully. Hector is indicating that I should skip side to side in a wide circle and to periodically reverse direction. He tells me to hold my arms upright. I dutifully obey and try not to get winded during the endless three-minute rounds.

The aerobic energy needed to run a marathon—pacing yourself for extended periods on asphalt—is initially useless in boxing, where short, sharp bursts of anaerobic energy are needed for rapid advances and retreats, side-to-side dodging, and tracking. Trained to run, I'm conditioned only to move forward, and as I skip sideways on the soft surface of the ring, I'm conscious of my weak ankles, which are threatening to fold under me.

Mercifully, the round ends, but Hector doesn't give me any time to rest. "Mix it up. Go forwar', back, side to side," he commands. I lumber about for four rounds before Hector finally waves me back out of the ring. "You move good," he says, walking me over to a stretch of wall covered in mirrors. He finds my wraps and gestures for me to hold out my hands, marveling at their large size, their prominent knuckles. I smile, for the first time, proud of their length and breadth.

Muhammad Ali's trainer, Angelo Dundee, says the key to wrapping a fighter's hands "is not puttin' it up front, like loading your fist, that's baloney . . . you're not making a lethal weapon, you're protecting the fighter's hands." Dundee would wrap Muhammad Ali's surprisingly fragile hands with sanitary napkins, because of his protruding knuckles.

Hector wraps my hands swiftly and efficiently, his skill so comforting and sure that it's almost like a massage; relaxing yet stimulating. He deftly shifts my fingers, snapping and unwrapping the length of cotton cloth and folding it or flattening it just so, to ease it between my fingers, around my wrist, across my palms. There isn't a single spot where the wraps feel too tight or too loose. He pulls the last twelve inches around and around my wrist, so the Velcro closure of the wrap will lie flat and out of my way. I silently revel at how good this feels.

Now Hector asks me to assume a boxer's stance. My first impulse is to put up my "dukes"—that is, raise my fists and plant my feet slightly wider than a shoulder's width apart. But keeping your feet parallel and beneath your shoulders is a critical mistake. A simple shove would knock you off balance. Mark had shown me how placing the left foot in front and the right slightly back creates a bracing effect against any backward momentum. While it looks like boxers face each other, they keep their torsos angled slightly away, to provide a smaller target. And so it's with knowledge and confidence that I assume this time-honored position.

Hector throws up his hands in disgust. "No! No no no! No' tha' way."

I try again, this time pulling my hands closer and higher, to protect my face, but he groans so loudly that I immediately drop them again.

"No' so high!" He makes a pinched face, balls up his hands, and presses them up to his face, blinking like a rabbit, by way of showing me how I look. I try again.

"No!" he barks, but now he grabs my arms and positions them properly.

Am I so far off? I study my wavy reflection in the cheap mirror ten feet in front of me. Okay, hands not so high, but not so low, either. My palms face me, my left arm angled out a little, not crimped too close to the body. He shoves my feet around on the thin, frayed carpet until they form a broken L shape, with my body in between. Satisfied, he then tells me to "walk aroun'," then return to that stance. I do, proud of my ability to isolate muscles, to reproduce form, to mimic poses.

"No!" he yells. "No' like that!" He kicks my left foot back an inch or two and slams my right elbow back into my side. He gestures that I should walk around again and resume the position.

"No!"

I stare at the mirror, dumbfounded, while he makes the smallest adjustments. I feel like I'm in a dance class with the great Balanchine; a millimeter off, and he's deeply offended. He tells me to move toward him. I take a step.

"Move forward!" he says. I take another. "No, jus' move!"

Eventually it becomes clear that I'm never supposed to move my foot heel to toe. I must pick it up and move it almost as a whole piece. To be rocked back on your heel is to be momentarily unbalanced, ripe for a fall. Hector tells me to move in this fashion, side to side, back to front. I practice this in the mirror, while he stands studying me, his brow furrowed. I feel my shoulders aching from the effort of holding my hands in exactly the right way.

Hector takes up two oval-shaped mitts and places them on his hands. Mark and I have done this before, so I know exactly what to do when he tells me to jab.

"No, no' like that." This time he is a bit more gentle.

It turns out that I fling my elbow out too far when I throw a jab. I try again, and again, to simultaneously shoot my arm out straight, keeping my elbow close to my body while turning my fist. This fist-turning action is "like turning a key," as an ex-boxer I once met described it. Now I throw a right.

"Good!" he says. After so much abuse, I take in the compliment greedily, resisting the urge to turn and see if the many onlookers who have taken in my faults witnessed this one moment of triumph.

"Wan—" Hector prompts, expectantly. "Wan—!" he says again, gesturing at my left hand.

One. I throw a jab.

"Two!" says Hector. I throw a right. We go back and forth like this for a while, until he sweeps his arm through the air as if to cut off my head. "Squash," he says, when I don't move.

Squash? My ignorance of Spanish is frustrating to us both.

He sweeps his arm again. This time I duck.

"No!"

I finally gather, after more pantomime, that I've leaned forward without bending my knees. Again, bad balance. He wants me to duck down simply by bending my knees and keeping my upper body in the exact same position. "Like that," he says, sweeping his arms back and forth. "Squash!

"Squash!

"Squash!

"Squash!" My thighs begin to tremble. My arms are beat, mostly from the tension of maintaining the correct position, and now my legs are quickly turning to mush. How could this be happening? I ran the Marathon!

An hour has passed. Hector unties my gloves, the bell signals the end of a round, and we walk to the speed bag area.

From movies to the latest sports coverage of a defending champ preparing for the big fight, boxers are shown whipping the speed bag into a blur as proof that they're ready to fight. On this day, I learn how easy it is to set the bag into motion, and how impossible it is for a novice to hit it once it begins swinging.

Hector shows me to hit the bag with the fleshy part of the outside of my fist, the edge of my hand, rather than my knuckles. "Go slow," he says, hitting the bag lightly and letting it bounce back once before hitting it again. He watches my clumsy efforts and, satisfied that I have the idea, says, "Three round," and walks back to his office. Since the bell signaling the end of a round has already sounded, I wait until the next bell rings before beginning. To start this new enterprise when everyone in the gym is resting would mean more people with the leisure to watch me flounder.

Hitting the bag in this methodical way (BANG bang bang BANG bang bang) is all I can manage, and soon, I realize that responding to the sound of its rebound is the key to success. Like drumming your fingers against a tabletop, you don't look down at your hands, you hear and feel their rhythm. Once I concentrate on using the bag to produce a consistent rhythm, my mistakes decrease.

After three rounds, I unhook the bag and walk back to Hector. He takes it and hands me a jump rope. "Two round." Both mentally and physically drained, I skip slowly, wondering if I'm risking a reprimand, but none comes. When I finish, Hector waves me over to a table covered in duct tape. He quickly pulls the wraps off my hands, then gestures for me to lie down with one leg bent, one leg straight. He bears down on my straight leg with both of his arms. I understand that I'm to do a sit-up. After twenty, we switch legs. I strain against his weight on me, against the pull in my lower back. Then he tells me to reach around and hold the table edge behind my head with both hands.

"Raise your legs up. Up up up! Keep them straight!" When I achieve pike position, Hector grabs my ankles and throws my legs to the table with incredible force. "Again!" I raise them up, he throws them down. He tosses them to the left, right, center. I grapple with the table edge, my hands sweaty. In any other gym, this would be considered unsafe: the way to throw your back out. I say nothing, of course, concentrating instead on breathing and relaxing with the force of Hector's aggression, trying to keep the workload centered on my abdominals. Suddenly he stops. He smacks my stomach.

"You think you conditioned?" he says with a smirk.

"It's . . . different. Than running." I'm trying not to gasp.

"Push-ups," he says. "Ten."

I execute ten nearly perfect straight-leg push-ups, then stand, trying not to stagger with the blood rush, and see that Hector was talking to another boxer and was barely paying attention to me. He's rolled my wraps back up into tight bundles and hands them over to me, along with my gloves.

"Ho-kay! Tha's it!"

I hope the smile on my face helps to telegraph exhilaration

and perhaps even surprise that the lesson is over so soon. Trying to impress my trainer and prove myself worthy of his respect is emotionally draining as well as physically exhausting.

"See you Wednesday," I say cheerfully. "Same time?"

"Yes, same time. No' so busy this time. Morning, very busy."

Back in the locker room, beads of sweat are trickling down my scalp to the end of my braid, soaking my back. Dropping my gear, I feel my hands still shaking from exertion. When I finally manage to open my locker, my clothes fall off the hook and spill to the floor. It's a tremendous effort to even contemplate picking them up.

But underneath that profound exhaustion, I walk down the stairs and out of Gleason's feeling recklessly giddy, as if I've impulsively signed a lease on an apartment that may be costlier than I can afford.

THE FLINCH

TWO YOUNG BLACK boxers are sparring in the ring next to mine. Though they're slick with sweat, every movement seems effortless and sure. Their heads neatly dodge every punch, their footwork is graceful. They're quick, they're lethal, they're tireless. I, on the other hand, am trying to avoid Hector's mitts, which are swarming around me like bats. I'm supposed to hit them, but every cell in my body is screaming for me to get away from this aggressive man wearing giant leather paddles on his hands before one of the mitts swings into my face. Each time he shifts his arms, I flinch. The day a boxer stops flinching is the day his skill becomes second nature. Months will pass before this happens to me.

"Look at your stance!" Hector bellows. Now he mocks me: arms bent awkwardly, blinking madly behind his fists, flinching all the while. We're focusing on the uppercut, the punch used to catch an opponent on the underside of his jaw. At home I've been studying a videotape of the collected fights of Mike Tyson and have noted that when he ducks under a wild swing, he rises with an uppercut. His closely held fist jams under the chin of his opponent, who collapses backward like a felled tree. But learning to throw an uppercut into an angled mitt is confusing. What part of the glove should make contact. The tip? The flat part on the top of my hand? A quick twisting of the wrist is involved in an uppercut, and I'm either doing it too late or too early for the punch to carry any power.

Burning with embarrassment at his caricature, I stand in a mockery of male bravado, shoulders squared, legs planted. The boxers to my left are working out on the heavy bags but occasionally glance over to see how well or how poorly I'm taking this abuse: *Will she cry?*

My feminine habit of cocking my hips and leaning on one leg is a liability in the ring; Hector points at my leg in exasperation, and I straighten my pelvis and redistribute my weight as evenly as possible. He raises his mitts, and my arms are readied. Exhaling for more power, I throw a left and a right; the right lands poorly, skidding sidelong on his left mitt. Then, in the second between punches, Hector takes a swipe at my exposed ribs.

Startled, I leap backward, stumbling a bit, and his mitt misses, cutting short his cry of triumph. He glares at me, cheated.

"Tha's a good move," he says. "You got some talent, and you used it." Actual praise! I can't help myself and giggle with pleasure.

"You think this is funny?" Hector says, glaring mightily. "Why you laughing?"

"Nothing, I'm just . . ." My voice trails off. Resetting my face into the stoic mask of the boxers surrounding me, I affect an expression of cool, dispassionate concentration.

Hector swings his arm toward my head as the lesson progresses; instead of "squashing," I'm supposed to quickly raise my forearm upward and block his roundhouse punch. He raises the mitt quickly from below, as if he's throwing an uppercut, and I'm supposed to quickly bang my forearm down to block that as well, in a sort of kung fu chop. But whenever I see his mitt hurtling toward my head, I flinch.

"Stop that!" he says, imitating me, all blinks and screwed-up forehead.

"Hit hard!" Hector says, holding up the mitts. When I slam out a one-two, he makes a whistling noise. "You hit hard!"

"Yeah?" The giggle is repressed, but a smile creeps

around my mouth. "When do you think I'll be ready to fight?"

"Nine months we kick butt."

My heart leaps at this news, since I was half expecting him to say, "What you talkin' about! Never!"

The bell rings. "Come on," says Hector, removing his mitts. He ducks under the ropes and jumps down to floor level. I do the same. Walking over to the steel cabinet outside his office, he replaces the mitts and retrieves a plastic bottle filled with water. He pulls out the bottle cap's nozzle, and I see that I'm supposed to open my mouth and tip my head back slightly. My instinct is to take the bottle from him, but outside the ring, boxing gloves mean helplessness, an inability to pick up or hold anything.

Hector pours just enough water for me to swallow a mouthful. Then again. Not a drop is spilled. While I stand and drink, he reaches over and adjusts my tank top, pulling it down and smoothing the ragged hem. The shirt was too long, so I cut it short with scissors. The hem keeps rolling up, and now Hector frowns. It's not perfect.

A gloved boxer requires help with nearly everything other than fighting, and trainers can be like mothers fussing over newborns when it comes to tending them. After hands are wrapped and gloves are tied, trainers adjust their clothes, wipe their faces, and tend to their many unspoken needs. Unspoken, since most trainers prefer boxers to be as mute as possible. And working with Hector, as with many other good trainers, is an odd mixture of care, nurturing, and goading, bullying abuse. I'm thirsty, but hesitate to ask for another drink of water. Hector sees me looking at the bottle, though. "More?" He tips it toward my open waiting mouth.

The bell rings again. Now we go to the heavy bags, something entirely new. Standing expectantly, I wait for his instruction, but I should have known it would never come.

"Jus' do it," he says, breaking the silence.

"But . . ." There are now several pairs of eyes on me; other boxers are working the heavy bags swaying around us.

"Jus' do it!" he insists.

I do it.

"No no no! When you can't hit, stop. When you can, hit!"

What?

I'm blundering along, throwing jabs. The bag swings wildly.

"Move aroun'," he says, and I glance over for more of an explanation.

"Don' look over here! Where you punching? Look where you fighting! Move aroun'!"

"Like this?" I ask, moving to my right.

"Yes!" he says, exasperated. "Keep punching!"

Okay, keep fighting while moving around the bag. Mercifully, the bell rings. Hector's constant exasperation makes me feel stupid. His patronizing tone suggests he's corrected my same mistakes a thousand times. So who has more patience? Me, for not screaming at Hector or Hector, for teaching a beginner? I'd complain, but if I did Hector would only think I'm "cryin'" because he's too tough. That's not going to happen.

The boxers who train with Hector barely look at me; I'm beneath consideration. Everyone else stares with a mix of curiosity, lust, and condescension. I think constantly about justifying myself to the room at large. Being capable and highly competent at all times is the cornerstone of my self-confidence, and suddenly being the least adaptable, the least knowledgeable person in the room makes me feel lost. I want to explain that I just started boxing, that I ran the New York Marathon, that I have a successful career.

When we move to the speed bag, Hector urges me to vary my punches, not just left, right, left, right, but four lefts in a row, then four rights, back and forth. Concentrating on new rhythms, I find a groove and begin to enjoy myself; as the speed bag is about restraint and timing rather than strength and power, it's a slight respite in the workout. The bell rings, and while pacing around, I spy a small wooden platform near one of the speed bag stations. It's for shorter boxers, a way for them to get higher up to the bag. Sitting down on it, my legs tingle with relief.

"Hey, no no. Don't do that."

This from a mustachioed man with greasy hair over in the weight-training area.

"No sitting down in Gleason's."

I laugh politely in response and remain where I am.

"No sitting down. No one sits."

It dawns on me that he's not kidding, and I stand up quickly before Hector sees me from across the room. Perhaps it was my panicked movement that alerted him, because now he's watching me nervously pace around. I raise my arm in a gesture of reassurance, and now, satisfied that all is as it should be, he turns his attention elsewhere.

"Are you fighting in the Golden Gloves?"

"No, I just started." Suddenly, Hector is right there.

"Don't talk to her!" He says it again in Spanish. I smile gratefully at Hector for rescuing me. But he glares at me before striding away again. I focus hard on a ray of sunlight that illuminates the leather seam of the speed bag. Then I relax my arms and wait for the bell to ring. I'm glad that Hector watches out for me.

At the end of my lesson, my ankles and feet are sore from skipping side to side. My choice of Asics cross-training sneakers may not be the best for boxing, and so I do what I've always done: ask my trainer for professional advice.

"What kind of shoes should I get?"

"You can get those," he says, pointing to a kid in Nike black high-top basketball sneakers. "They look good. Or wrestling shoes. Or boxing shoes. You have long legs, so they'd look good." Bruce passes by, and I nod and smile, indicating all is well.

"Well, I don't care about looking good, I want the best shoes."

Hector is flabbergasted. "Looking good is very important for a boxer! Very important!"

Bruce perks up at this and stops to voice his agreement.

"What would you think of me if I didn't look good?" says Hector. I see that he has chosen his outfit with care, the matching athletic pants and billowing zip-up jacket, the gold chain with the giant gold boxing gloves dangling from it, something I later learn is the winner's trophy from a fight in the Golden Gloves. "Everyone look at you, see you style!"

One scan of the gym, and I see that my frayed T-shirt is actually a faux pas here, the equivalent of jeans at a black-tie dinner. Here, to dress well for your workout is a matter of status, about wearing your wealth. I wonder how many of these boxers have large gold rings, necklaces, and bracelets carefully stored in their lockers.

"You must look flashy!" Hector goes on. "Have personality! Look good on TV! See him?" Hector is pointing at a bellowing ox of a man who is shoving around a heavy bag, leaning on it and pushing it almost as much as hitting it. "He fight Mike Tyson!" Indeed, this boxer is in a green satin jacket and matching pants, black boxing sneakers that climb up his shins, and ornate gold-framed tinted glasses.

A name is emblazoned on the back of the jacket—Mitch

"Blood" Green: the heavyweight who was once cold-cocked by Tyson, not in a ring, but late at night on a side-walk in front of a clothing store in Harlem. The bell rings, and Hector yells over to him, "You fight Tyson!" Green swaggers over.

"Mike Tyson," he says, "is a *puta*." He looks at me. Sweat pools on his cheeks around his glasses, the initials MG in gold flash in the corner of each lens. "You know what that means? Faggot." Hector laughs uproariously at this comment as he hands me my wraps and gloves. I manage a smile and walk away.

Once inside the locker room, I sink to the floor with my head against my knees.

————

At the start of my next lesson, Hector tells me to shadow-box in front of the large mirror, so I'm clumsily moving around, pawing slowly and self-consciously at the air. Joe Gatti, one of Hector's boxers, is shadowboxing just to my left, his body making tiny corkscrewing moves left and right, supporting his lightning-fast punches.

Both Joe and his younger brother, Arturo, train with Hector, and there are a few posters up on the walls commemorating Arturo's title bouts. I heard from Bruce that Joe, though not as successful as his brother, is training for some big fight this summer. A good-looking man with soulful brown eyes and shiny dark hair, he favors immaculate white trunks, white T-shirts, unscuffed sneakers, and fluffy white socks, a contrast to his evenly tanned skin. A closer look confirms shaved legs. Last week, he left the gym in a shirt that looked fresh out of the box, neatly pressed pants, hair carefully slicked back.

"Where you headgear?" Hector interrupts my shadow-boxing.

"At home," I say, somewhat abashed. My locker was so crowded, and since I wouldn't be needing the headgear for months, I took it home with me.

"What you do with it at home?"

"I don't know, Hector," I say wearily. "I thought I'd cook with it."

"Cook with it!" He's not smiling. I tough it out.

"I didn't think I'd need it for a while."

While Hector and I bicker, Joe's still in front of the mirror, his muscles rippling under his smooth golden skin. His feet dance around as he throws combinations in the mirror. Surely Hector doesn't expect me to spar with *him*. Not without headgear.

"Ho-kay. You spar with Joe. Get in the ring and move aroun'."

Panic. A rise of adrenaline shoots from my feet to my face. This is a real boxer, a man bigger than I am, stronger, completely experienced. Everything. He'll tear my head off without even staining his pristine T-shirt.

"I need a mouthguard," I blurt out. "I'll be right back." Darting into the women's room, I tear open my locker. It's still in its plastic envelope, with the instructions on how to mold it to your teeth. There's a diagram on how to soften the plastic guard in a pot of boiled water before biting down on it. Good Lord, why didn't I do this already? Racing back out to Hector, I hold out the package helplessly.

He looks at me, furious, then storms into his office to plug in an immersion coil that he uses to make instant coffee and tea. While it sizzles in a cup of water, Hector rips open the package and studies the instructions. He dips the clear plastic in the hot water and removes it with a spoon.

"Take it!"

I take it and pop the steaming plastic in my mouth.

"Bite down! Then don't move."

The corners of the guard pinch hard against my gums in the back of my mouth around my molars. "Come on!" Hector says. "Waste time!"

He grabs my gloves and shoves them on my fists. I can barely breathe with the guard in my mouth. Joe is still shadowboxing, relentlessly jabbing and pounding the air.

"What should I do?" I ask. The mouthpiece also slurs my speech.

"Move aroun', jab, jab, right, move aroun', move you head . . ." He looks at me as if this should be obvious.

Hector rattles off something to Joe in Spanish. Joe nods his head rapidly. With any luck, Hector is telling him not to break my ribs, that it's my first time sparring, and that I have no idea what I'm doing. Ducking down under the ropes, trying not to stare at the bloodstains, I still haven't figured out how to draw breath with my mouth closed, and I sound like a pig snorting. Neither one of us is wearing headgear. Cracking open my jaw a bit, I hyperventilate while we wait for the bell.

"Stan' up! No' tha' way!" Hector is pointing to my leg. As usual, I'm leaning on one more than the other. Straightening up, I roll my shoulders, a vain attempt at relaxation. Joe is dancing around. The bell rings.

Moving fast, I throw a jab as hard as I can right at his head.

"Hey!" says Joe with a laugh.

Ah! He's surprised at my prowess! Even though I missed, I surprised him!

Joe calls out to Hector, "She doesn't know about touching gloves?"

What?

"Jus' fight!" says Hector, annoyed at both of us.

Joe retreats and I advance, jabbing every few seconds, missing constantly. His head has moved out of the way long before my fist can ever make the long, slow journey from my chest. My exhalations around the mouthguard sound like a steam engine about to stall out. Joe whirls around me with more energy, and I'm panic-stricken at the thought of his fists coming anywhere near my body. I taste blood: a sharp edge of the mouthguard is pinned into the spot where my wisdom teeth used to be.

"Move aroun'!" Hector bellows, to whom I'm not sure. Joe effortlessly moves away, causing me to chase him to all corners of the ring, which leaves me too exhausted even to keep my arms properly upright. Following him as he retreats, I stare into his eyes, which are large, brown, and downturned like a spaniel puppy's.

"Throw you punches!"

Joe swivels his head back and forth, to and fro behind his gloves, as I try desperately to connect with a few swipes, a few glancing blows with my jab. Close enough to smell him, a wave of something weirdly familiar hits me. Then the bell rings.

I would be jubilant that I'm still standing if I had the energy. When I stagger over to Hector, he motions for me to open my mouth. Reaching in, he gingerly removes my mouthguard and with it a thin trail of saliva lands on his hand. This would be embarrassing if I had the strength to react. Is an apology for the drool appropriate? Hector holds the water bottle up, and my mouth opens wide.

"This is so tiring," I gasp between mouthfuls. Hector ignores me. I hadn't realized that when working at the heavy bag or practicing my form, there's a tiny bit of downtime. There's no downtime when you spar. Not only are those small rests removed during sparring, but in my case, that day, they were replaced by sheer panic.

"You wan' to stan' and fight, stan' and fight! But don' jus' stan' there! Move aroun' or throw punches." The bell rings. Lacking the nerve to simply beg for mercy, I manage a pleading look at Hector as he slides in my mouthguard.

"Fight!" Hector says, shooing me away.

Joe offers his gloves forward, and I see that we were supposed to have touched gloves before we sparred. I've seen boxers do that before a fight. Oh, of course! Why didn't Hector tell me? After our gloves meet, I take a leap backward, terrified he'll sucker punch me while at close range. Circling around, trying not to hyperventilate with fear, trying to calm down as Joe advances, I jab at him, flailing.

"Throw a right!"

Bracing myself for a terrible right hook, I stumble backward, arms raised against my face.

"Throw a right!" I look over to see that Hector's talking to *me*. "A right!" he screams. "Don' jus' stan' there! And don' look at me! Look where you fight!"

I swivel my head back around to Joe and fling out my right hand in an attempt at a punch. Joe bats it away hard, his glove smashing down on my right wrist. Nearly following my arm right down to the canvas, I switch to my other hand and throw a left. Joe smashes it away too, almost knocking me down. With both arms stinging, I step backward and move side to side to give them a chance to recover.

"Where you goin'?" yells Hector. "Go in and fight!" Joe's hands are up, poised. I'm terrified of him, but more afraid that Hector will call me a coward, so I quickly throw a one-two. The jab misses, and the right hits his glove, which doesn't move.

"Fight!" Hector screams.

I keep throwing punches at Joe's head but succeed only in hitting his gloves. An uppercut? But Joe's forearms seem to cover him from his stomach to his nose. Effortlessly, he bats my jabs away, which hurts like hell. I back up and drop my arms momentarily to get the blood flowing back in them. My forearms throb.

"Put up you gloves!" Hector yells, appalled. "Don' drop you hands! Fight! Fight!" Trying to look busy, I shuffle around as if I'm waiting for an opportunity to move in on Joe, but I am just swaying on my feet, desperate to stop. Joe's eyes stare out balefully through the gap between his gloves. Where's the bell? The thirty-second warning rang a week ago. I move in again, resigned to make an effort, and manage to slowly extend my glove out and tap Joe's forearm. The bell rings. Joe smiles and holds his gloves outstretched.

We touch gloves again. I'm mortified at my poor show-ing, but so utterly relieved that it's over and that I didn't pass out from exhaustion or get knocked down that I smile. I stagger over to Hector, who pulls out my mouthpiece. Now able to speak, I shout, "Joe! Thanks, I really appreci-ate you sparring with me."

"It's okay, you did good," he says. Drinking in this ca-sual comment, I smile in an attempt at modesty. When he turns to walk away, I nail the smell: *fabric softener.*

It's only later, when I'm at home, reconstructing the ex-perience in my head, that I realize Joe never raised a glove to me the whole time, nor did he plan to. *That's* why I was put in the ring without headgear. The reason Joe went in without headgear wasn't "to make it a fair fight," as I thought at the time (what was I *thinking?*), but because he, Hector, and everyone else in the gym knew that I'd never, ever manage to hit him in the head. Joe was put in the ring only to practice his defense.

Groaning with embarrassment at my complete misreading of the situation, I lay down on my sofa and buried my head in the pillows. It would be less humiliating if he had just knocked me out in the first round.

LEARNING TO BE VIOLENT

TWO MONTHS AFTER I start training at Gleason's, I bought tickets to the New York finals of the Golden Gloves. This was a much-heralded event, because 1995 was the first year women would be allowed to compete.

Most of the advance publicity about the significance of women boxing in the Golden Gloves focused on women wanting to know how to "defend themselves." For women, learning to fight is acceptable only if you're fighting back, and in boxing, that's not enough. When asked, the female competitors often described boxing as "fun," "a way to get out your frustrations," but not as something they had taken up as self-defense. This fine distinction was glossed over when it came time for the press to explain why women were taking up the sport. Reporters have long been reluctant to explore boxing as a sport that legally sanctions the pleasure men derive from expressing their violent impulses, so I wasn't surprised that they would avoid examining this obvious motive when it came to the women.

This evening's event takes place at the Paramount Theater in Madison Square Garden, and I've brought along Mark Loader, an old friend and fight aficionado. This venue is more often used as a concert hall; the seats are plush and placed on a slight rake, and the stage is dwarfed by a high ceiling, gently curved for acoustic reasons. In showcasing a sporting event, the room's elegance is wasted and finally serves to remind the crowd of the gracelessness of the spectacle before them.

With a gin and tonic in my hand from the bar in the lobby, Mark and I settle in and make side bets in our programs. We decide to arbitrarily select opposing boxers to cheer on, and whoever wins the match owes the other a dollar. While our seats aren't exactly in the cheap sections in the back, neither are we situated in the good spots down in front; at times, we strain to see the details of the action in the ring.

The very first Golden Gloves tournament was held in Chicago in 1923. The championships can be likened to a beauty pageant, where boxers, like beauty queens, must win several smaller competitions before they can compete at the regional and then national levels. The stated purpose of the Golden Gloves is "to promote amateur boxing as a positive lifestyle for today's youth," but in reality it serves as a pipeline for professional boxers. Past winners have included Muhammad Ali (as Cassius Clay), Joe Lewis, Charles "Sonny" Liston, Jerry Quarry, Michael Spinks, Sugar Ray Leonard, Oscar De La Hoya, Evander Holyfield, and Mike Tyson.

Despite the esteemed history of the championships, most of the matches in the finals that evening could hardly be called boxing. Amateurs with varying degrees of skill veered between street-style violence and slapstick. Two barely trained fighters bolted out of their corners like racehorses, ramming into each other with such force that they both fell to the ground. Others threw wild roundhouse punches that never connected to their more experienced opponent, who dodged or simply waited calmly for the opportunity to deliver a quick, bout-ending punch.

The bell rings, and two women charge out of their corners, one frantically throwing punches at the air, the other running with both gloved hands held straight out like battering rams. This is a sharp contrast to the traditional style of male boxing, where two men, their fists raised, hop and step cagily around the ring, assessing each other's strengths and weaknesses, before actually coming to blows. The women here aren't defending themselves, studying their opponents, or even boxing: they're wreaking havoc.

Even as I judge these women, I cringe at the idea that my own performance could be as embarrassing to watch.

A few fights into the program, a group of men sits down behind us, talking and joking loudly. These are big beefy men in their late twenties, early thirties (they could be off-duty cops or firefighters), mostly mustachioed, with thinning hair and burgeoning bellies beneath muscular builds just starting to sag. As they shift past to their seats, a few jostle the backs of our chairs. Grumbling a protest, I turn around, but the group is too busy getting settled to notice.

The evening wears on, and we see three bloody noses and two outbursts from the crowd over the judges' decisions; my chair back is kicked and bumped with every shift and exit to, or return from, the bathroom or snack bar. One of the men behind us, broad-shouldered with curly reddish hair, announces he's making a beer run for his buddies. As he exits the row, he grabs the back of my chair for support and, in the process, accidentally pulls a lock of my hair with his hand. I yelp with pain; he releases his hand as he murmurs, "Sorry there," and moves on.

"These guys are driving me crazy," I say to Mark, who, in the way of a guy who wants to avoid a physical challenge, is studiously pretending that everything's fine. At six foot five, Mark looks far more imposing than what he actually is, which is a fairly shy, polite Englishman. I whisper, "Someone bumps my chair one more time . . ." Mark chuckles dismissively.

While I sit and stew, this same man returns with four

large cups of beer. Eyes front, I grit my teeth and wait for the inevitable jostle. Then it happens. A cold stream of liquid hits my neck and cascades down my back. Jerking upright, I stand, wheeling around in the cramped quarters so fast, I almost pitch forward over the back of my own seat.

"Beer!" I blurt out. The spill is clearly a mistake, another accident of sheer carelessness, but just then, to my horror and amazement, my hand, which was clenched into a fist around my program, shoots out and strikes him, hard, in the chest, in a well-executed jab. The beer from four paper cups sloshes against his navy blue polo shirt, making a large dark wet stain. Taking my punch, he has no place to put the beer down, and no hands free with which to fight back. He turns his shoulder, offering a biceps like a canned ham, a shield to protect the drinks and his shirt.

"Down my neck! Apologize! Beer!"

My arms are flailing in frustration, and while I don't have the nerve to hit him again, it's impossible to tamp down this release of physical aggression now that it's been jump-started. I whack him across the expanse of his freckled arm with the rolled-up program. Twice.

"Hey! Sorry! I'm sorry!" he says in a mix of surprise, chagrin, and anger. His friends have been laughing at the sight of their pal, helpless, being hit by a woman. I bore into them with an intense expression that I fervently hope conveys the depth of my fury. "You guys have been bumping my seat all night, and now I have to get beer in my hair? *I don't think so.*"

One of them says, "Ooooh. She should be in the ring, right, Mikey?"

"Just watch it, okay?" Trying to deescalate to the realm of cool and casual, I turn back around. I'm overheated and my heart is racing, and the first prickles of embarrassment move in with my awareness of the high number of smirking onlookers. People are staring. Mark, for his part, is acting as if there's something extremely unusual in the program, an item that has his full attention.

"Christ!" Mark mutters, still staring at the page. "Leave me out of this, okay?"

"Don't worry about it," I say, mortified. Still, I'm annoyed that he thinks I would expect him to step in on my behalf, as if he's my protector. Someone taps me on the shoulder. I spin around, braced. A man two rows back is leaning down to pass me some napkins. Murmuring my thanks, I pat my hair and wipe my neck.

For the rest of the evening we endure the taunts and running commentary of the guys behind us. "Yo, Steve, does she hit harder than your wife?"

"She should get into the ring. Hey Steve, why don't you get in the ring with her? No beer this time."

"Oh yeah, I was scared. I'm still scared. She'd scare anybody with that face."

I pretend not to hear or care. All I can think of is this: *Once violence is learned, it cannot be unlearned.* Before Gleason's, I'd had three options during an argument. Walk or run away, wage a war with words, or surrender and make peace. But now a fourth option has suddenly presented it-self: my fists. Before I even considered the question *Is this a good idea or a bad idea?* or even made a split-second as-sessment of my chances, as in *Can I take this guy in a fight?* I had already jabbed him in the chest. My brain had, on its own instinctual level, adopted a "shoot first, ask questions later" policy.

The most brutal fight we see that night is between two women, Tanya Dean and Sekka Scher, both in the 165-pound weight class. According to the program notes, Dean trains at "New Bed-Stuy BC" (Bedford-Stuyvesant is a dangerous neighborhood in Brooklyn; BC would be short-hand for Boxing Club) and works as "a corrections officer." Scher trains at the "Wall Street BC" and works for "a mar-keting firm on Wall Street." It also mentions that Scher "used to ice-skate a lot." Mark and I exchange glances be-fore the bell rings. "Dean," we say in unison, neither one of us willing to place a dollar bet on Scher.

We are not the only ones to feel that way. The crowd is on its feet the minute the fight starts, sure that Dean would mop the floor with her opponent. We aren't wrong. Dean is much quicker than Scher, and her blows, for the most part, land squarely, many of them in Scher's face. But what keeps the crowd on its feet is the fact that Scher keeps box-ing. At moments when any of us would crumple or run, she keeps coming back for more. In between each round, Scher's face, covered in blood from a nosebleed, is wiped and her headgear is adjusted, and when the bell rings, her resolve to stand up and face her opponent never falters. In the third and final round, I am convinced that the crowd, and even Dean, is praying for her to just lie down. Our will to witness her struggle is not nearly as strong as her will to fight. But she goes "the distance." Dean is declared the winner.

Unlike the majority of the male boxers, all female competitors hug after their fights. Scher and Dean cling to each other in an emotional embrace, hanging on, pulling back, only to rejoin again in a tearful hug of thanks, or perhaps relief that their ordeal is over.

The crowd, which usually spares the loser its cheers, cheers as loudly for Scher as for Dean. In an evening of mostly shabby amateur performances, Scher has displayed that quality most prized in boxers: heart. It's more than bravery or a lack of cowardice; it's the will to fight and go on, even, and especially, when you're losing. Or maybe it's a failure to see reason, a dearth of common sense in blind pursuit of a grand heroic gesture.

At the end of the evening, when the fights are over, a man bounds up the stairs toward us. He's short and broad-shouldered and has a shaved head. He extends his hand in my direction. "Hey!" he says, happy to see me. At first I don't recognize him, but then I realize that he's a guy I've seen at Gleason's, sparring, talking to other boxers. He usually wears a stocking cap; it's strange seeing him without it. We've never spoken before, and it's jarring to see him here, in the same way it seems odd to run into your teacher on the street. We shake hands briefly, and he takes off toward the exit.

"Who was that?" asks Mark.

"A guy who goes to my gym. He's another boxer." *Another boxer.* It slips out, the recognition that I have somehow graduated from the status of civilian spectator. Mark and I are fussing with our coats and belongings, delaying our exit so we won't have to walk out next to the guys in the row behind us. Neither of us mentions this as the reason; it just seems terribly important to inventory the contents of our pockets, to examine the buttons on our jackets for signs of wear, to carefully roll up our programs before finally heading outside.

I walk out of Madison Square Garden, shaken by what I've done and what I've witnessed, wondering where heart ends and stupidity begins. And whether summoning the will to walk the fine line that divides the two would mercifully spare me from knowing I had slipped to the wrong side.

HEART

IN JUNE 1980, Roberto Duran, a street-savvy Panamanian, won the WBC welterweight crown after beating the undefeated Sugar Ray Leonard. Five months later he stunned
the boxing world by ending their rematch with the words
"No ma's." No more. Turning away from Leonard, he simply stopped fighting in the eighth round; his disgrace
would last for years. He had lost the will to go on. In the
world of boxing, this is known as having no heart.

Hector is unlacing my gloves after I've gone three rounds
with Cesar, a thin, wiry Hispanic guy in his mid-twenties.

"Thees guy," says Hector, shaking his head and smiling briefly, "no heart." This pronouncement about my sparring partner is depressing, since I was expecting Hector to tell me that I fought well against a formidable opponent.

This is, however, the first time Hector has mentioned heart. This brings on a new fear: that Hector will think I don't have any. I need to press Hector for specifics, to seek clues that will help me avoid Cesar's predicament.

"No heart?" I say, taking a speed bag from Hector's equipment locker.

"He scared! Run from you!"

"I thought I just did better today."

"He knows you can hit, so he run away!"

"But it's good to run sometimes. Why does that mean he's scared?"

"He scared! Run from you!"

Once Hector starts to repeat himself, no further information is forthcoming, and I remain confused about the difference between cowardly running and wise evasive action. The language barrier makes such fine distinctions nearly impossible to explain, so I walk away with the speed bag before he can accuse me of wasting time with chitchat.

Cesar is skipping rope. He has a flattened nose, one that's been broken a few times, a sculpturally interesting addition to what would be a rather ordinary long face. He's wearing black tights with thin white stripes that are more appropriate in a dance studio than a boxing gym, but the macho touch of a sweatshirt with the sleeves ripped off allows some compensation. He's skipping and nods his head in my direction. Drumming steadily on the speed bag, I wonder if Hector is right.

When Cesar introduced himself to me two weeks ago, he had sparkle in his light brown eyes and a small, amused smile on his face. Still in street clothes, he shook my gloved hand in what could pass for a clumsy yet courtly gesture. In sharp contrast to the monosyllabic encounters typical to Gleason's, he tried to engage me with his many questions: where are you from, where do you live, how long have you boxed, and why do you like boxing?

"Do you have any children?" he once asked with a smile.

"No," I said, stunned, wondering what might have given him that impression.

"Okay," he said with a light shrug. It took a few months of hearing this same query to understand that most of the men here at Gleason's don't know any childless women. Asking a woman about her kids is an easy icebreaker, and to find out that I don't have any is a surprise.

When Cesar and I stepped into the ring together that day, he seemed torn between demonstrating his prowess as a fighter and behaving like a gentleman.

"Don' hit her in the face," Hector told him as we waited for the bell to sound. I wondered if Hector spoke English to Cesar because he thought his near lack of accent meant he didn't understand Spanish. "I don' wan' to break her spirit."

With Hector's admonishment, my confidence grew, and as the buzzer went off, I approached Cesar with what I thought was a steady eye, a good stance, and calm assurance. That's when Cesar hit me hard. In the ribs. This is a stunning, heart-stopping, lung-shriveling moment, where the only option for recovery is to fold up. My diaphragm wrenched back into action, and air flew back into my lungs. I gasped like a beached fish. But Cesar kept on coming at me. One, two, three punches to my ribs. Doubled over into a near crouch, with both of my arms across my chest, my gloves under my chin, I was trying to move backward and out of his line of fire, but my legs were rubbery with the effort of holding my body upright. This was a vivid lesson in why shots to the body are so debilitating, physically and emotionally. Unable to breathe in or out or to move, I was still able to grasp the humiliation and extent of the disaster, an experience I might have been spared if he had hit me in the head.

"Fight! Defen' youself! Move you hands!" Hector bellowed, furious that I had now dropped them and was attempting to stand upright. Normally, this is a fatal mistake, one that gives your opponent a clear path to your jaw, but since I knew Cesar wasn't supposed to hit me in the face, I risked the exposure. Cesar, satisfied with my obvious incapacitation, could now afford to be the gentleman and backed off. I looked up at him with something like gratitude.

"Move aroun', hit, hit, move aroun'," Hector urged. Regaining some breath, I moved in and hit Cesar as hard as possible with a left jab. I had aimed at his face, but he saw it coming in time to get partially clear; my fist slammed into his headgear. I threw a right into his chest, which was covered by his forearm, and then he was back all over me with a flurry of punches to my body. By the time the bell rang, any semblance of gratitude was long gone; I was glaring at him like a cornered cat. It went on like this for three rounds. When he left the gym that day, he smiled jauntily and waved at me as if he'd just won a bet.

Today, when I see that Hector is pairing the two of us together again for sparring, I brace myself for the worst. As Hector slides in my mouthpiece, I'm already hyperventilating in anticipation of the assault I'll have to launch the second we touch gloves. I know my only chance will be to hit him with absolutely everything I have right away, before I get winded and tired from the beating he is about to give me.

Panicked, my punches are wild and unschooled, but I am desperate to protect my ribs. I am frustrated, too, that Cesar keeps backing away, that I have to waste so much energy chasing him around the ring. He wears an expression of worried concentration, as if he is holding a thrashing salmon on the end of his fishing line and doesn't know how to reel it in without losing it. Cesar was going to wear me out without laying a hand on me.

Still, I hit him whenever I get the chance. By the third round, if Hector and some cronies weren't watching and shouting, I would have simply mirrored Cesar's circular travels. When the final bell sounds and I climb out of the ring, Hector seems oddly joyful. And that's when he starts chuckling.

"Thees guy, no heart."

There are complex issues at stake when a man enters a ring in order to box a woman. Trouncing a woman is a hollow victory, akin to beating a child. But for her to beat you means you haven't just lost a boxing match, you've surrendered your manhood. Maybe Cesar's just not comfortable with a lose-lose proposition. Did he feel bad after brutalizing me a couple of weeks ago and vow never to repeat it?

In retrospect, Cesar gave me my first glimpse of what fear can do in a boxing ring. For some men, losing any ground to a woman is so unacceptable that they lash out in anticipation of her first punch. Cesar's brutal assault the first time we sparred was completely out of proportion to any threat from me. He gave me everything he had immediately to ensure that I would never throw a punch that could knock him out or humiliate him. When he backed off while I was incapacitated, he didn't want to risk cornering me; I might have been frightened into an adrenaline-fueled attack. If he stayed too close to me, he just might fall victim to a superhuman uppercut. Better to dance backward, view my recovery from a safe distance, and move in again when he sensed an easy opening.

The second time we sparred there was something else.

As usual, before sparring, Hector drilled me with his mitt-covered hands for a few rounds.

"Wan, two." A jab and a right. *Thwack thwack.* "Hit hard," he admonished. "Wan!" he commanded again. I planted one as hard as I could. He nodded. "You hit hard!" He had looked over at Cesar to make sure he heard that, still nodding at its significance. At the time, I thought this boosting of my abilities was for my benefit. After all, Cesar totally dominated me last time and barely broke a sweat. But now, as Hector holds down my ankles while I count off sit-ups, I consider the possibility that I really *do* hit hard.

Standing up, I see Cesar heading for the door, freshly showered, carrying his gym bag. I deliberately cross his path, and our eyes meet for a moment, but he raises no hand in greeting. He looks momentarily startled, as if he were lost in thought and my presence reminds him of an unpleasant chore. He passes me without a word. I have my answer: this guy, no heart.

Later that day, when I'm at home and reaching for something in the refrigerator, I notice the marks on my hands for the first time. Large purple and red bruises have bloomed across each knuckle. I turn on my desk lamp, for closer inspection, examining my hands underneath the bright glare. The darkest area, plum-colored, extends down the finger from the knuckle above the pinky on my left hand. A streak of red suggests a spot where the wraps bit into my flesh, and I can see that my desperate jabs were landing with most of their force on my little finger, instead of the flat part of my fist. I'll have to work on that, I think, as I touch the other bruises on each knuckle and feel the swollen flesh, the jellied sensation of water beneath skin.

At that moment, in my kitchen, a memory-door opens and a face from twenty-five years ago appears in my head. Mark Antonelli.

Mark was a sullen twelve-year-old boy who looked as if he never combed his hair. I first saw him at the start of the school year. He had a broken jaw, which was wired shut, a glamorous temporary affliction in sixth grade when two scabby knees was a mark of bravado and a cast on a limb was an automatic pass for extra privileges. I later heard this injury was the result of a car accident over Labor Day. I've since wondered if it was actually the result of family violence. At the time, it would have been inconceivable to imagine that he might have been a victim of violence himself, so wrapped up was I in my own anxiety over being the new kid in school once again.

My family had just moved to Pennsylvania from Virginia. My father was a naval officer, and I had heard a million times that when it came to being the new kid, my older brother, Rob, nine years my senior, "had it far worse," since he was in grade school during the part of my dad's career when it meant a transfer nearly every year. At age eleven, our move to Norristown, where Dad was to be stationed at the Philadelphia Navy Yard, was only my fourth.

Mark was the one, since there's always one, who waited

in the school cafeteria until I passed him with a tray full of food. He was standing with three of his friends, the usual pack of sycophants who are attracted to bullies like remoras to sharks, and all three wore the impatient, agitated expressions of those easily bored and easily entertained. I heard snickering behind me but was far more preoccupied with where or with whom I was going to sit. I scanned the room through my glasses, which had slid down my nose that critical quarter of an inch. I didn't have a free hand to push them back—the tray was too heavy. Where was the girl who lived across the street? Or the one I spoke to that morning who seemed friendly? Walking ever so slowly with my tray, I felt horribly conspicuous and prayed that there would be seats available with people I barely knew, that they would look up and wave me in. Kids I might have seen in a crowded hallway or on the bus that morning looked up at me with the momentary curiosity of trying to place a face, and, just as quickly, turned away, distracted by their tablemates or their food. Suddenly, during this agonizing search for a safe haven, two hands delivered a hard, well-timed shove into my back, just between my shoulder blades.

The tray flew from my hands and went into free fall. My arms windmilled, my legs splayed shakily. A heavy plate hit the floor with a horrible clatter, breaking neatly in half. Gravy splashed upward on my shoes and knee socks, but I was grateful to remain upright. My face was tingling with embarrassment, the sensation of hot needles dancing on my skin. I thought I was safe from tears if I only looked down on the wreck that was my lunch. This moment, when tiny cubes of precut vegetables briefly rose into the air like miniature fireworks before falling back down to the floor, was my introduction to the entire student body at Penn Square.

There was an explosion of laughter, a prolonged howling ululation that must, in any grade school, follow the crash of a lunch tray. I glanced up briefly and saw my math teacher glaring at me in exasperation. Too embarrassed to go up for seconds, I stood by (where would I sit? and with whom, after this humiliating display?) while a man in a hairnet came out and swept up the mess.

Mark and his friends came into my sightlines; they were now in the seats to my right, the front-row view of the disaster. Mark was grinning at me as much as he could with his teeth wired together. His friends were red-faced with excitement and glee, doing everything but patting him on the back. I remember Mark laughing, making snorting, snuffling noises like a muzzled dog. That shove was just the beginning for him, a warm-up, his test for a new patsy.

Walking to my closet, I dig around in a box for my Polaroid camera. Holding each of my hands as far from the lens as possible, I take two pictures of the damage and write "Cesar" on each of them: trophies. Then I fill two Ziploc bags with ice, head for the sofa, and drape them across both hands. I look down at my hands with new respect and massage and stroke each bruise with reverence.

I can still hear Mark laughing over my ruined lunch, but now I sock him hard in the left temple, and boy, is he ever surprised. "You like to pick on girls, Mark? How does that feel?" His hands fly up to his face to ward off my blows, but they arrive too late; my fist has already made contact with the soft cartilage of his nose. I feel it crushing like a Styrofoam cup. I see the panic in his eyes as he crumples to the floor. A crowd has gathered, kids are jostling for position, eager to see but careful to maintain a safe distance. Wide-eyed, they gaze upon the fallen tyrant—and then up at me with respect and gratitude. I'm a dragon slayer, and I have prevailed.

FIRST BLOOD

THE BLOOD IS not my own. It's Tommy's, and it's oozing out of his nose in an irregular path toward his upper lip, the legacy of one of my punches. Tommy is a classic Irish-looking fighter, more brawn than muscle, standing at something like five foot ten, with a pug's face offset by pale blue eyes. Tommy boxes methodically, his fists gently pinwheeling the air as he considers his next move; he approaches slowly and cautiously, out of respect for my inexperience. Or perhaps his hesitancy can be better explained by the fact that Tommy is in his mid-fifties, with snow-white hair poking out of his well-worn headgear. It's round two, and when I see the blood, I pause to glance at the few spectators. Surely someone—maybe even Hector, or perhaps Gigo, the dark, brooding man who acts as Hector's assistant—will stop the fight. My elderly opponent may actually be hurt!

The bell rings, and we retreat to our corners. It's a dreary March day, the air in Gleason's is stagnant and humid. I left my usual cotton tank top back in my locker, and now, with only a sleeveless, shorts-length, black jersey unitard, I realize the true function of a cotton T-shirt: a makeshift towel between rounds. As I pour with sweat, Hector removes my mouthpiece, and I open wide for the water he's poised to squirt in.

"You stan' there, throw punches!" he says as I greedily swallow. "You pushing you punches, fight bam, bam, bam. Pull you arm back! You snap the jab!"

"He has a bloody nose," I gasp out.

"And keep you elbow in!" He shoves my arm for emphasis.

"His nose is bloody. I hit him in the nose. It's bleeding." He looks over. Tommy's face is being wiped; the towel shows a smudge of red near one ragged corner.

"Hey!" Hector yells over to Tommy. "You bleeding?" Without waiting for an answer, Hector laughs and claps me on the shoulder. "Punch him in the face," he says, shoving my mouthguard back in. The bell rings.

Tommy has apparently received exactly the same advice,

and directly after we touch gloves, he neatly lands a left hook over my eye. Now is the time to pull my hands up to protect myself, but the effort seems too great, the logistics too complicated to execute in a split second, so I dumbly wait for his fist to rocket into my temple. Then it happens; a strange noise implodes inside my skull, a dull roar, a muffled shattering, a sound like something falling and striking the floor. I don't see stars, or planets, but there's a definite impression that a plug has been kicked out of its socket. I take a heavy step sideways to stop myself from falling.

Tommy takes advantage of my dazed condition and lands two more shots. Even in my addled state, I note that he chose not to aim for my face but the side of my head.

"Move aroun'!" Hector yells. I dutifully hop backward and start varying my footwork, hoping that Tommy isn't one of those energetic fighters who will follow too closely. But he's manning his spot, the wisdom of experience telling him that to chase me will wear him out, and that he should avoid the arena of endurance, a young man's game. We both know that if he draws me back to him, he'll stand and fight me off. Treading canvas on the opposite side of the ring, I regain my breath. For both of us to hold our ground is beginning to look ridiculous; it's not much of a fight with Tommy pinwheeling his arms at a standstill and me hopping gently side to side, a wide gulf of ten feet safely between us. Hector is again yelling his usual advice: "Jab, jab, move aroun'!"

I dance forward and throw a jab that connects solidly to

his jaw. His flesh mashes beneath my glove with an unexpected softness before I feel the bone beneath. Tommy's head rockets back. For a moment, I'm incredulous. Didn't he hear Hector instruct me to do just that? I dance backward again.

"What you doing?" Hector is apoplectic. "Hit! Jab, right!"

Cutting a glance over to Hector, I can't believe he's watching the same fight I'm currently in. What I really want to do is shriek, "I hit him! Didn't you see his head move back like that?"

I throw a combination of five punches, and the first three land. Tommy fends me off and covers his head. After slamming a right against his forearm, I back away again, exhausted. The bell rings.

Hector's yanking out my mouthguard and scolding me simultaneously. "Stan' and fight! Protec' youself! Go in, jab, jab, go out, back and forth." He wipes my face with a towel and squirts more water into my mouth. I swallow and fight to speak before he puts my mouthpiece back in.

"I'm tired," I gasp out.

"Tired!" He looks shocked.

"I hit him in the face again. He's hurt." This last gambit is part fishing expedition and part distraction; I didn't like the look on Hector's face when he heard I was tired. He looked disgusted, incredulous, and amused all at once. After all, I was fighting an old man!

The fact that I'm winded within three minutes is

disgusting to me as well. To a distance runner, three minutes is a nanosecond, the length of a heartbeat. In a boxing ring, pain and fear stretch time, and as each second elongates, ordinary sounds distort to a low, dim roar of a distant ocean, a hive of bees.

The bell rings, the mouthpiece is resolutely shoved back in; discussion over. I inhale in jagged breaths, as usual fighting to breathe with a huge piece of plastic in the way, and confront Tommy again.

He looks as if he's sagging on his feet, content to take it easy for this last round. When our eyes meet, his seem to widen as if asking a question. I blink back in what I hope appears to be the answer he's looking for: a discreet signal that I'm tired as well, let's just get through this and hope that no one gets hurt. Or more to the point, that I don't get hurt. I blink a few more times: *Please don't hurt me. I'm a girl.*

No deal. Tommy lands a punch directly into my nose and mouth, which has been hanging open slightly in an effort to get more air past the mouthpiece. "Shit!" I blurt out, astonished. "Fuck!" The lower half of my face is going numb, and my armpits are tingling. Saliva pools in my mouth; I'll drown if I don't spit out my mouthpiece. I back way off and pop the unwieldy bit of plastic forward a little, just past my molars. It's now jutting out of my mouth, and my tongue is squirming around in the effort to corral the spit. I fight the urge to retch.

"Put you hands up!" Hector shouts. "Up! Fight!" I can't.

The mental concentration needed to reposition my mouth-piece is overwhelming. My head is killing me, the throbbing pain hurts the very roots of my hair. I rub my ribs with my gloves as if they're hurt and buy a second or two more of rest. Sucking my mouthpiece back in, I dance toward Tommy, jabbing at him. He blinks and shakes his head, as if to clear it. Then suddenly he throws a right, and I dance backward as if his glove is electrified, nearly tripping over my own feet, but he misses me. There's a metallic taste in my mouth, something like copper: blood. I'm biting down so hard on my mouthpiece that it's cutting into my gums. The warning bell sounds at last. Rallied by the knowledge that it's almost over, I stride toward Tommy. His eyes have narrowed to bitter slits. Terrified that he's plotting another blow to my skull, I practically run my outstretched left arm into his head. He ducks and pulls his head down low, but I'm on top of him now, and my right comes up hard in an uppercut, catching his face. Leaning forward, I trap his head, grabbing it from behind with my left. We're in a clinch, his headgear is pressed so closely to my nose, I can smell his scalp, an unpleasant intimate moment, as my mind catalogs sebum, grease, smoke. I thrash my arm a little, struggling for another hit, too afraid to let go. Hector is yelling something, but I can't make it out; I think Tommy has his glove over my ear. We're locked together like this, and I don't care that his head is shoved into my breasts, I just don't want him to be able to hit my face anymore.

The bell finally sounds, and we go limp. I cautiously

relax and back off. Tommy picks his head up, and there's blood on his lips, draining steadily from his nose. He's saying something, and I can see blood in his mouth, on his mouthpiece, on his teeth. I'm transfixed for a moment, before turning away. On my way back to my corner, I glance down to see if there's blood on my chest, but the black makes it hard to see. At least there's none on my skin. Walking over to Hector, I spit out my mouthpiece into his hand and smile.

"You did good," he says. "You have to hold you hand up, jab, jab, move aroun'."

I look over at Tommy. "Thanks," I tell him. He nods courteously, a bit of a smile lingering. He looks rueful: better to let the woman win than to beat her? Or perhaps it's the regret that he's fought punks for so many years and this is how he ends up on a windy March afternoon in Brooklyn: a bloody nose from a woman.

"Am I bleeding?" I ask Hector as he takes off my headgear. It suddenly occurs to me that the warm wet feeling around my mouth is blood.

"What? No!"

"I'd hate to get a bloody nose. You look like you lost the fight."

"No," he says, as I step out of the ring, "you get bloody nose, people say you tough guy."

As we walk toward Hector's equipment locker, I see some boxers clustered together, looking over at Tommy and laughing a little. Arturo Gatti, Joe's brother, is shaking his head, smirking, looking from me to Tommy and back again. I recognize him from the fight poster behind him; the same flattened face with a large sturdy jaw, a human version of a pit bull. Joe is actually better looking, but Hector has bragged about Arturo's looks and talent as if he's responsible for both. Arturo smiles and raises his glove slightly toward me.

If you have a bloody nose, people aren't going to say you're a tough guy if you were hit by a woman.

DREAD

I LOVE MY apartment and its order. I always make my bed in the morning, my desk is spotless, my books are arranged by size. And on top of my file cabinet is the lone island of whimsy: my toys. When my young nephew Chris visits me, he's amazed by them. He doesn't know any adults who still have an Etch-A-Sketch. I also own a Magic 8 Ball, a Rubik's Cube, a Freddy Krueger glove, and a stuffed-shark hand puppet. I use these mostly when I'm at my desk, "working." My other prized possession is my red

Princess telephone, which my father gave me when I went to college.

My father learned how to fly in a biplane and ended his thirty-year career landing jets on aircraft carriers. To me, he was the man who knew everything—how to fix a toaster, how to dig a well, how to build a split-rail fence. He was the one person who always made me feel safe. The night after my fight with Tommy, I called him on my red telephone and asked if he had ever been afraid.

"Sure," he said. "Many times!" I was surprised at the ease with which he admitted this.

"Was it during the war?"

"Nah. I was invincible then."

"But death was right around the corner! You never thought about that?"

"See, I knew I was good at flying. It was around the corner, but not for me. I always worried if I had to take a test. If there was a test for promotion. I still have bad dreams about taking tests."

This is so laughably mundane, I can hardly stand it. "You mean the dream where you don't have pencils, or there's only two minutes left in the test period, or you've never taken the class—"

"Yes! Do you have those dreams too?" He sounds worried, as if he's passed on these dreams as a family legacy. After assuring him that I don't dream about tests, I steer the conversation back to landing a jet on an aircraft carrier at night; was he really never scared?

From a quarter mile away, the carrier appears to be the size of a pinball machine on a football field, a tiny flat skillet that is in constant forward motion, bucking and rolling on top of giant waves. In the dark, there's only the stars, the instrument panel, the voice on the headset. I can picture this so vividly that I imagine being too scared to land, and I wonder if that fear would be stronger than the alternative: running out of jet fuel, ejecting, having to explain the loss of a $20 million aircraft.

"Before flying at night, I always thought, 'I could walk away from this right now. Just say I don't want to do it, and I won't have to.' "

"They would let you do that?"

"You'd have to appear before a board. At one point, I sat on that board. And we'd hear pilots who would say, 'I don't want to fly at night.' We'd say, 'You don't want to fly at night? What do you want to do, tow targets?' And you could always tell which guys were going to drop out, as far back as preflight school."

"What would happen to them?"

"We'd tell them that we're going to have to take their wings!"

"Would any of them cry?"

There's a silence on the other end. My father has choked

up momentarily. When his voice comes on the line again, it's hoarse and trembles a bit.

"Wouldn't you?"

"I'd rather crash the plane than say I wouldn't fly at night."

He pauses again and lets out his breath. "Me too. Of course."

I hang up the phone and realize, for the first time, how similar we are. I would rather get beaten to a pulp, week in, week out, in this struggle to improve, to do well, to know what it is to be capably violent, than admit I'm too scared to go back.

The walk to Gleason's gym in Brooklyn from the nearest subway station is, fortunately, mostly downhill. I appreciate that small fact of geography over the hundreds of times I make that walk, with slow, tentative steps, willing myself to descend.

I usually stop at a small park along the way, where the gardens are well tended. I admire the profusion of crocuses, tulips, daffodils, and lilies and watch the sparrows search for bits of food, pecking in the mulch. On beautiful days, and even on rainy cold days, I envy the sparrows the way a child envies a sibling who is allowed to stay home from school. At some point I know I will walk away from them, enter a building, climb into a ring, and get the crap beaten out of me. And even on the days when I'm not sparring, if I pass the subway station that I use to travel to Brooklyn, my heart begins to pound inside my chest.

A few shots to the ribs and face have made me lose perspective entirely. Dread of future body blows and escalating violence to my body have put me on the defensive, as much out of the ring as in.

At a dinner party, an actress tells me we have something in common: she attends a boxing class at her gym. I interrupt her litany about her cute instructor with all of the subtlety of a left hook: "See, what I do involves *combat*. What you're doing is acting as if going to *boot camp* is the same thing as seeing *action* in a *war*. You take a boxing class, but it's not *boxing*. You're learning some sort of skills that you never put into practice, so how can you even say you know how to do it? Hitting a heavy bag is just *practice* for hitting a person! It's like knowing how to use a steering wheel without ever getting into a car, and telling people that you know how to *drive*!" Other guests at the table have stopped talking, and I look down at my plate. The pale peach sleeves of my dress contrast sharply with my bruised knuckles.

"No, you're right," she says, her lip curled, "I'm not doing that. But why would I want to?"

"Because it's fun," I say, smiling. *Liar.*

To her, what I'm doing is foolhardy. And as I repeat this performance at dozens of parties, I'm aware of the large chip on my shoulder. I can't bear that she doesn't know what it really feels like to have someone hit you hard, with malicious intent. The real answers are so complex and sound so preposterous. *I'm full of rage and I want to beat someone up. I want to know what it is to have physical power over men. I want to inspire fear. I want to matter.*

Why don't I just quit?

I'd rather crash the plane.

ATLANTIC CITY

HECTOR IS PLANNING to drive two of his boxers down to fight in Atlantic City. Knowing that my parents live in neighboring Margate, he asks if I would like to get a ride down and back with him over a weekend in late April. That way I could visit with my parents and also take in the fights at Bally's Casino. Raymond Joval and Arturo Gatti are scheduled to fight in two different bouts on the same card, and Hector will be there as their cornerman. And so on Friday afternoon, clad in a maroon business suit with a red silk shirt, I walk into Gleason's with a small overnight bag.

Hector gave me a ringside ticket to the fight yesterday. The cost of the ticket was thirty-five dollars. "I'll reimburse you for this."

"No!" Hector was firm. "You my guest!" I offered again, and he angrily refused: "I got thees for you!"

Something about his tone made me uneasy. I've developed an instinct born of experience to be wary of invitations where strings might be attached, of an offer made by a man who might want something from me in return that I'm not prepared to give. And so when Hector offers me a free ticket to the fight, I hesitate, wondering if the price to be exacted will turn out to be much higher than the thirty-five dollars in cash I wish he would accept. Perhaps the ticket is complimentary (one that he's passing on to me, but no such story, and the reassurance that I'm now off the hook, is forthcoming), or perhaps Hector was acting in an old-school Latin way, where a woman is simply never permitted to pay for anything, or perhaps he was simply being generous. "Thank you," I said finally. He nodded gruffly and waved me, the ungracious one, away.

The plan is for us to leave following an afternoon workout, in order to be at Bally's by early evening for the weigh-in. Despite my trepidation concerning the ticket, I'm looking forward to the trip.

Having now agreed to go, the next hurdle is how I will be perceived. For while Hector, with his limited English, surly demeanor, hefty build, and murky marital status—his wife and children live in Panama, occasionally a young son comes to visit—certainly isn't my idea of a dream date, I'm not comfortable with the idea of being seen as anybody's date.

Almost a year has passed since my husband and I separated, and I am, to my astonishment, actually seeing someone. We met through a mutual friend in the film industry, when we, and several other people, were asked to appear in a sound room to dub background voices for a party scene. Eli is younger than I am and works for a film producer. He's wiry and easygoing, with a terrific sense of humor. Plus, he's athletic and can keep up with me on my six-mile runs in the park. Even though we're seeing each other exclusively, he understands not to refer to me in any way as his "girlfriend," a parameter that strikes me now as the superstitious demand of a woman desperate to hold on to her heart. He's flattered by my interest and eager to comply with the strange wishes of a much more accomplished older woman. I, in turn, am thrilled by the attentions of a much younger man, one with few demands and refreshingly little emotional baggage.

Standing in front of my closet, I wonder how to send my message of autonomy through clothing alone. I settle on two business suits: one for the weigh-in, one for the fight. Either outfit would be appropriate for a day in court or a presentation in a boardroom.

Changing in the locker room, I fuss with my suit, the one hook suddenly inadequate for the job of clothes management. My thoughts in this room have always been about which boxers I've passed on my way in, and who I'll likely be paired with once I emerge. Today brings a new set of concerns: squeezing my bag in will mean crushing the pants; and what are the chances of someone coming in here and stealing anything if I set my bag outside my locker? A tall twentysomething woman with long medium-brown hair wordlessly passes me in here as if I'm the dumb new kid, even though she's the one who trains with Angel, the guy who trains only women—that is, dilettantes who don't want to get hurt. She's not going to bother my bag, and neither will that stockily built thirtysomething woman with the short dark hair who seems pleasant enough. My hand hesitates on the locker door when considering the heavyset teenage girl who once remarked to someone as I passed, "She's too stuck-up to box me. She's scared." Hector, along with the other trainers, has refused to work with her until she sheds some weight. Her anger and resentment over the fact that I'm being trained by Hector might mean that leaving my bag out in the open here might be too much of a temptation for her. Forcing the bag into my locker, I carefully wedge the door shut and close the padlock.

I spot Raymond Joval shadowboxing at the mirror as I emerge from the locker room. Tall and handsome, with rippling muscles and high cheekbones, his face seems gentle in repose but frightening once he lowers his head like a bull about to charge, setting his eyebrows, clenching his jaw. A few spectators are watching him run through combinations, bludgeoning an invisible opponent. He looks well prepared, rested, and utterly lethal. "I don't want to hurt you before your big fight tomorrow, so we probably shouldn't spar today." I risk this joke as a point of pride.

"I fight you anytime," he says calmly. Originally from Africa, Raymond's family emigrated to Holland, and he boxed on the team from the Netherlands in the '92 Olympics. A middleweight, he moved to New York in the hope of earning the big money by shedding his amateur status. After sparring with him several times, I've come to appreciate his professionalism: a man who can handle boxing an inexperienced woman without letting the fear that she'll land a "lucky" punch goad him into an over-the-top display of brutality.

Raymond's ego is still large enough that he needs me to be in some pain after a fight with him, but sparring with him is less frightening knowing his punishment is all business and nothing personal. While we've never discussed it (Ray's accent and vocabulary make most conversations difficult), he can be trusted not to cross a line beyond what I can take and still remain standing. His hard and fast jabs to my sides are enough to make me cry out, but they aren't powerful enough to break my ribs; a blow to my face is aimed at my cheekbone, which is more comfortably protected by the headgear, rather than at my nose, vulnerable and inviting. Some sparring partners are unpleasantly surprised by the power behind one of my punches, and they retaliate in an all-out assault before remembering that I'm half their weight, half their size. Raymond has never let his emotional response to a punch make him lose control.

Hector pairs us together to spar. After he announces this, I say, "So, I should just take it easy on him, right?" Hector remains stone-faced as he laces up my gloves.

"Jab, jab, move aroun'. Use you hands. Don' push you punches. Bap bap bap."

The bell rings, we touch gloves. Raymond has his fight face on, a terrible laser-eyed glower coming at me through his headgear. I try for the same expression as we dance around as an easy warm-up, but it's clear that Ray isn't affected; he was just practicing his fight face and barely notices what I do. He allows me to throw some punches in his direction so he can practice his ducking and weaving. Nothing I throw connects, and something in my right elbow pops as I hyperextend my arm in a spectacular miss to his bobbing head.

In round two, Ray continues to work on his defense, chopping down my forearms the moment my punches are halfway near him. With legs rapidly turning into cement blocks, I chase him around the ring. Each change of direction stresses the balls of my feet; they feel like two hot coals in my shoes. By round three, just keeping my arms up is a full-time job, but Hector is yelling at me to throw more punches. Leaning into a punch as if my arm is holding a door against an intruder, I funnel all of my strength and energy down my forearm and into my glove. My fist lands on Ray's two upraised forearms, which are as immovable as two stone pillars. There's nothing so disheartening as watching your best effort sputter and die. The bell rings. Ray paces and glowers at me as I take my leave, and Hector sends in what everyone watching thinks of as a real sparring partner, another middleweight. I'm sent off to work out on the heavy bag, the jump rope, and the speed bag and do sit-ups under the mute observation of Gigo, Hector's assistant.

Like Hector, Gigo is Panamanian, stockily built, and of an indeterminate age. His grasp of English is even more tenuous than Hector's, but his silence reads more like wariness, as if I'm someone who won't be here in a few weeks and therefore isn't worth his time or coaching.

After the workout, it's time for what's known as a "birdbath" in the locker room. I picked up this term after overhearing one boxer remark to another about someone's poor hygiene: "I seen him just takin' a birdbath in the sink! I told him, that's no shower, man." Maybe not, but it's something between being sweaty and enduring a trip into dank horror at the end of the room. Carefully unbraiding my hair, which is dripping with sweat, I let the cold water run over my head for a few minutes. Splashing water and soap around my body, then patting myself dry using several paper towels from the roll I have stashed in my locker, my hair is combed out, deodorant applied, the suit buttoned up. Dressed up and ready to leave town, I wait near the exit door, bag in hand, for Hector and Raymond to emerge from the men's locker room.

As I pretend to be absorbed in the view through the window, harmless taunts from boxers—"Where you goin'? Can I come too? You stayin' at my house?"—fall on deaf ears. If I waited facing the gym, it would signal my readiness to engage in what passes for conversation, and the number of men with similar inquiries would triple. These men are flexing their heterosexuality for one another rather than for me, so ignoring their entreaties isn't a snub.

"Where's Arturo?" I ask as we walk out. Raymond is in a form-fitting, thin black sweater and dark pants. Hector is in beige pants and a dark, patterned V-neck pullover. His large gold chain with the boxing gloves pendant rests against his exposed chest. He's pulling on a lightweight white zip-up jacket, slashed across the chest with triangular panels of shamrock green and navy blue.

"He meet us there." This is a disappointment, since my best chance for conversation is with Arturo, who can speak English fluently. Since talking seems to be forbidden between Hector's boxers inside Gleason's, I had imagined this car ride might finally give us all an opportunity to get to know one another, beyond boxing. If there is anything beyond boxing.

Across the street is Hector's car, a shiny, very clean dark green two-door sedan. "You take the front," says Raymond. "I can stretch out in the back." He's boxing tomorrow and should be spared the stiffness from a long car trip which leaves me to sit up front, with Hector. Raymond refuses to discuss switching seats. He's far more concerned about what to do with his freshly dry-cleaned and pressed silk boxing trunks. He opts to lay them carefully on the back-seat, arranging the plastic of the dry-cleaning bag so the striped fabric remains flat. The choice of tangerine orange and white, explains Raymond, is from "the colors of the Dutch flag." A thick black waistband is adorned with a white JOVAL like an oversized belt buckle.

Shortly after the drive begins, a sharp turn deposits the precious cargo onto the floor. He hangs it up, draping the plastic over his outstretched legs. He still seems cramped, so I scoot my chair forward as far as possible. Over the course of our drive, Ray periodically reaches over to reassure himself that his trunks aren't bunching anywhere. Ray confesses that his main concern for tomorrow is the possibility of having to box a full six-round fight, which would be his longest bout ever, yet he seems far more worried that his outfit will get wrinkled before we get there.

I hate casinos. I worked in the purchasing office at Caesars in Atlantic City for a summer during college and later worked as a cocktail waitress at the Tropicana in Las Vegas. The noise, the smell, the patrons themselves—the expressions on their faces a mixture of hope and defeat—are profoundly depressing. Bally's is no different. We arrive with no time to spare before the weigh-in. Crossing quickly through the casino floor, our senses are assaulted by buzzers, bells, the steady metallic drone of coins being emptied into aluminum trays, and the tinny musical notes played by hundreds of slot machines. The air, though smoke-free, has the stale, recycled stench of a commercial jet after a cross-country flight.

In Gleason's my outfit was too provocative, in Bally's it's too elegant. Nearly every gambler is wearing a windbreaker, a jogging suit, or a baseball cap, athletic gear being the preferred uniform of nonathletes. Hector strides ahead of us through the crowd, clearly disdainful of gambling, shaking his head at the people laying down their money.

"Stupid," he says. "No respect for themselves!" I nod in agreement; there seems to be very little joy, even among winners, in a casino.

Raymond is quiet, preoccupied, content to follow along. After traveling up an escalator and wandering down several hallways and shopping areas, Hector sees someone he knows and shouts a greeting. A thick-necked man with unnaturally dark slicked-back hair raises a beefy arm in return and points down a hallway toward the press room, where Arturo is just leaving with his manager. Arturo doesn't recognize me for a moment, but then he does and appears to be confused as to why I'm there at all. He looks me up and down as if the answer to my presence might be found in my outfit. Could he think I was there as Hector's date? The thought is mortifying. He and his manager head off to dinner. Arturo always has a problem getting his weight down before a fight, so he's undoubtedly starving.

The press room is tiny, a bland, low-ceilinged meeting room in the hotel, filled with a few long tables, a scale up on a pedestal, and the hangers-on of the boxing world: the pinky-ring-wearing promoters and managers with pock-marked faces who claim a "piece" of one boxer or another, grizzled trainers, and jaded, well-worn members of the press, taking notes by hand, picking at dirty fingernails between interviews.

As the only woman in the room, I'm conspicuous, and any hopes that my outfit would eliminate ideas of a romantic involvement with Hector are quickly dashed by his waffling, ambiguous nonintroduction. After warmly greeting Lou Duva, the bearlike grand old man and legendary leather-faced trainer of such champions as Evander Holyfield and Pernell Whitaker, Hector sees my expectant expression and adds, with a gesture toward me that seems a little embarrassed, "My friend . . ." before letting his voice trail off.

"I'm Lynn Snowden," I say, proffering a hand for a firm, all-business handshake. "I'm one of Hector's boxers." Duva gives me a tight little smile, another crease to his lined face, as if he doesn't believe a word of what I've just said. "It's a real pleasure to meet you, Mr. Duva," I add, but his attention is already elsewhere. Hector says hello to a few other people, and I try out a number of titles for myself after Hector mumbles "My friend . . ."

"Hello, I'm one of Hector's associates."

"I'm a client of Hector's."

"I currently train under Hector."

No one is interested. Suit or not, I'm Hector's date. What's particularly annoying is that out of everything I might be to Hector, "friend" is not one of them.

With his back to me, Raymond quickly strips down to what looks like a black jockstrap. My eyes alight on his perfectly curved hamstring, and my gaze travels up to take in a smooth, dark, tightly packed gluteus. It's only then I realize I'm seeing Ray's naked butt. My eyes widen with shock: did the whole room see me staring? I had forgotten that stripping down at the weigh-in, sometimes entirely, is one of the traditions of boxing. Embarrassed by this unasked-for intimacy with Ray, I walk away from the pedestal as he steps up on the scale.

"One hundred sixty pounds." Photographers are taking pictures, so I sneak a glance; Raymond's flexing his arms and smiling, his lower torso thankfully shielded by the people in front of him. He quickly dresses, and I saunter back over as if my leaving the area were sheer coincidence. Hector suggests we join Arturo for dinner.

"I really have to call my parents. In fact, I was supposed to call them the second we got here. They're going to be worried."

"You call, go to dinner. Then I drive you to your parents'."

"No, it's okay, my dad can come get me." Suddenly, dinner seems more than I can stand. After the encounter with Arturo, and miffed that Hector didn't introduce me as if I were a real boxer, and angry that perhaps he was correct in this distinction, my mood has soured.

"Come on, let's go," Raymond whines.

There's a pay phone in the hall. I stop and wave them on, but Hector waits, standing close as I dial the number.

"Dad!" Glancing over at Hector, I see he's staring into my eyes, offering no provision for privacy. "Yes! We made it fine. Listen, I'm going to just get a little something to eat here, unless Mom has something all prepared already and doesn't want me to ruin my appetite."

Praying that my father will pick up on the cue that I need an out, I curse myself for never devising a code word for "I need assistance." Considering the careful, suspicious nature of my father, an ex-military man to boot, I'm surprised he didn't devise one for me years ago.

"Listen, you do whatever you need to do. We can hold dinner here no problem. Eat there if you like." Can Hector hear his side of the conversation? It's possible.

"I know how Mom gets really mad if I miss one of her meals." This isn't true: maybe it will jar him into realizing that something's wrong.

"Oh, I'm sure she'll be fine. You take your time there. We'll see you whenever you get here." Hector grunts in satisfaction as I hang up the phone, and we go on to the restaurant, a diner-type eatery set up cafeteria style.

As we sit down, faint strains of Muzak warble over tinny stereo speakers: "Bridge Over Troubled Water." This is the downmarket restaurant in the casino, the place for losers and low rollers. Boxers competing tomorrow get a free meal.

Arturo and his manager are sitting at a small table across the room and make no effort to join us. I cut into my soggy beef stew and listen to Raymond's theories on food.

"Before a fight, I eat chicken, pasta, vegetables, whatever I want."

"What do you avoid eating?" I ask, but Ray looks at me blankly. Vocabulary. "What's not good to eat before a fight?"

"Pasta. Too much pasta. Or too much meat. Chicken."

Letting the discrepancies slide, I let Ray ramble, since he seems so relaxed now. It's the most he's said all day.

With dinner over, Ray goes to his room. Hector, who insisted on paying for my meal, moves toward the elevators rather than the exit.

"So now we get the car and go to my parents' house, right? It's not real far away. It'll take us five, ten minutes."

"I wan' to go to my room first. Drop my bag."

"I'll wait here."

"You come upstairs, you don' need to wait here. Where you going to wait here?" We're standing in a hallway lined with shops selling sweaters encrusted in rhinestones, garishly patterned silk scarves. Casino hotels are notorious for not providing any place to sit unless it's in front of a dealer or slot machine. The welcoming tone of Hector's voice suggests that I'm being silly. Maybe I am being silly; the man just wants to drop off his bag. Being alone in a hotel room with Hector suggests an intimacy I don't want him to be able to claim with me, but I can stand in the hallway when he drops his bag.

"You min' if I take a shower?" he says, opening his bag on the bed. He sets a large bottle of Bacardi Limon rum on the night table. Hovering near the door, I die a little at this new development.

"I really have to get to my parents' house. In fact, you shower, I'll go downstairs, and my dad can come get me. You've been driving all afternoon, and it's a big imposition. It's fine, really. You relax, I'll go."

"You sit down, I shower, five minutes, we go to you parents'." He sees me step into the hall, already reaching to pull the door shut behind me. "You bag. Suitcase."

Blinking, I'm not sure what he means for a second, and then it's obvious: I left my bag in the trunk of his car. At this moment, the bed fills the room. Any remaining space is taken up by the unsmiling Hector.

"Okay," I say, not wanting to offend him. "Five minutes, then we really have to leave. Really. Or my dad will just show up here. No kidding." With that, Hector takes some items into the bathroom with him, including a small shaving kit. The room is a riot of greens and grays, and the fireproof fabrics of the drapes and bedspread are slick and shiny.

Sitting in the only chair, it's clear that the possibility of relaxing, even for a moment, is slight. Another image suddenly crowds in: the girl who accused Mike Tyson of rape.

The beauty pageant contestant who came up to his hotel room late one night. At the time this was in the news, my friends focused on how stupid the girl was to put herself in that position—alone in a hotel room with *Mike Tyson*! They assumed she must have been interested, or incredibly naïve not to know that he didn't ask her up there to discuss philosophy. I once worked as a volunteer at a rape crisis center and it was shocking to hear so many victims use the phrase "I didn't want to be rude."

The shower water is running: not ten feet away, Hector is naked. What would a jury, the police, the public, say about my circumstances right now? Witnesses saw me with Hector at the weigh-in, and most of them would say I seemed happy to be with him, and that they had assumed I was his date. Considering that Hector is married with children, couldn't I be seen as a woman who accuses him of rape out of frustration that he won't leave his wife? Or are my worries that I'm about to be assaulted, taken against my will, part of being cautious, a residual paranoia left over from my days as a rape crisis counselor?

The water is turned off. I'm being silly, and it would be silly to offend Hector, who's just trying to be helpful. He paid for dinner and my ticket. And sure, that beauty pageant contestant probably didn't want to offend Iron Mike, either. Just as I'm debating the wisdom of leaving a note telling Hector I'll meet him at the valet parking area, the bathroom door opens.

To my immense relief, he is fully dressed, wearing dark

pants and a beige sweater. Hopping immediately to my feet, I'm nearly knocked back down by a wave of cologne, a cloying mixture of musk and something so artificially sweet, it makes my teeth ache. Stepping forward, Hector wraps his arms around me in something between a bear hug and a restraining hold; moving my arms or wriggling away is an impossibility. I shouldn't be shocked—but I am. He plants a kiss on my lips.

"You're my trainer!" I gasp. The worst has happened. Clearly, I can't escape. Who would hear me if I called for help? My only option was to talk myself out of this hideous situation.

He mumbles something about how this won't affect how he is in the ring with me, as if my concern at the moment has anything whatsoever to do with how we could juggle both a sexual relationship and a professional one.

"You don't kiss Arturo, or Raymond, or Joe, so you don't kiss me! I want you to treat me the same way you treat them."

His grip loosens only slightly. I change tactics. "This doesn't show any respect to my boyfriend!" As much as I hate the idea of being a man's property, I pray that Hector's perception of a male's wrath about his woman being violated might cause him to rethink his behavior. "Or my *father*! You don't show any respect for him, acting this way! And what about your wife and children?" He's dropped his arms and reaches for his coat and grabs the room key. I see he is furious: the wife and children remark may have pushed it too far. I head for the door and turn around as I grab the doorknob. He's right behind me, glaring mightily. Riding the elevator down in silence, he stares straight ahead. That I'm able to look over at him but he's not able to do the same makes me feel a tiny surge of power. He's ashamed. Or perhaps just humiliated by my rejection, and the initial fury because of it has passed. Emerging to a long line at valet parking, it's only then, out in the open, with people nearby, that I feel safe. Now I can afford the luxury of anger.

"*I* have respect for your wife. But *you* don't respect me when you do that." I am desperately trying to be clear. "I want a *trainer*. I *have* a boyfriend. Your job is to prepare me to fight. *Right?* You have to treat me with the same respect you show to Raymond." The car finally arrives. Our only conversation on the drive concerns directions. That he's still quiet emboldens me enough to press the issue.

"You're coming to meet my *parents*," I tell him. That seems to work, and he gets out of the car, meekly now, and retrieves my bag.

My dad is standing in the doorway. He's in his seventies but still has the bearing of a military man. The smile that lights up his face when he sees me makes me feel like I've truly come home.

"There you are! And you must be Hector! We've heard so much about you!" Hector returns his smile sheepishly and carefully wipes his feet several times on the doormat before stepping inside. I take the bag from him, satisfied with his nervousness. My mother gives him a kiss hello. She's a beautiful woman whose fresh-faced good looks helped her become the part-time model she was when she met my father. Still, she's something of a loner, not prone to doling out kisses to people she's just met. My parents fawn over Hector as if their politeness will safeguard their daughter from harm in the ring.

Seeing this ordinary middle-class house through Hector's eyes, I imagine it symbolizes prosperity, security, and authority: the brick mantelpiece, the fire in the fireplace, the white rug, modern furnishings, crystal glassware in the breakfront. The television is tuned in to an entertainment news segment, and my young nephew's photograph beams out from the glass coffee table. Quiet and cowed now, Hector is out of the conversational arena of boxing, and his English fails him. He demurs on the offer of a cocktail and says he must be going.

"What time should I drop her off for the fights?" asks my father.

Hector looks at me, unsure of both the question and the answer.

"Two o'clock. Like we said."

Hector nods, smiles, waves a little, and leaves. I collapse onto the couch, feeling that we've reached a stalemate; perhaps I've even achieved a small victory.

As I greedily suck down a glass of red wine, eager to feel the loosening of tension, I tell my parents everything. I sum up the evening's events with the observation that I should have known better, that I won't ever be so stupid as to meet Hector anywhere other than the gym. That I was coming down here with him lent a seriousness to my boxing career in their eyes, but suddenly Hector, the great boxing coach, has become Hector the Harasser. And instead of a serious boxer, I've become his victim. The two of them ask if there's anything I need, if there's anything they can do. Beyond that, they're at a loss, clearly shaken by this new development, even though I've downplayed the moment in the hotel room, more for my sake than theirs. I feel sick, angry, scared, apprehensive, and more than that, I'm afraid I'll have to quit. I reassure them that I've straightened everything out, it was just a big misunderstanding. The three of us have to believe that—me most of all—since underneath these emotions is the certainty that Hector is a great trainer. And despite everything, I still want to learn from him. He's given me the technique, and I'm feeling confident. I can envision the strong, fast, ruthless, and sure boxer that I could be if I trained a little harder, sparred a little longer. I'm so close to it now that it's easier to go forward than to quit and go back to the way I was: weak, helpless, powerless.

———

The next morning my father offers to escort me to the fights, but I'm going to have to deal with Hector sometime, and it might as well be now. So I walk into Bally's alone. The event is held in a large conference room, and the lights hanging above the ring seem uncomfortably close to the action. Boxers preparing for their fights rest on folding chairs set up in small, curtained areas, in temporary dressing rooms. "In cages!" Hector says to me when I arrive, far less subdued since the last time I saw him, renewed by the raging testosterone, the animal electricity in the air. It seems as if the previous day's events have been entirely forgotten.

I wish the fighters luck and make my way down to my seat, which is six rows from the ring. In the section next to mine, two curvaceous blondes in low-cut minidresses stand against their chairs, as if they're on a stage of their own. Hector points to them. One is Arturo's ex-girlfriend and is, according to Hector, the reason behind Arturo's distracted manner yesterday and today. He doesn't want her here watching him fight, and, Hector adds, "He don' wan' to be with no ol' lady." She's twenty-eight, Arturo is twenty-one.

A man in a brown business suit sits in the seat next to mine and introduces himself as Jerry Gormley.

"You're with Hector," he says.

"I'm one of his boxers."

"Don't be a boxer!" An ex-boxer himself, Gormley says he's now a lawyer in New York City. He sees me staring at scabs running across the knuckles of his left hand. "I got into a street fight yesterday." He amends this. "A mugging." He takes a deep breath. There's a manic energy to him. "A face mask might protect your looks, but not your brain. Think about it! The only way you can win in boxing is to separate someone from the one thing that distinguishes him from a dog or any other animal: a rational mind. Or to disfigure him physically, to maim him so the fight is stopped." He shakes his head. "Don't do it."

There are six fights on the card, and Raymond is in fight number four, going in with a perfect 9–0 record, 5 of them knockouts. His shorts are wrinkle-free, and he cuts a colorful figure with red gloves, purple and red boxing sneakers, and white socks trimmed with purple rings. His opponent, Earl Allen, looks strong, in a more dignified all-black outfit, with a shaved head and a light mustache, but has a less impressive record, with 4 wins, 3 draws, 2 losses, and 2 knockouts.

The two go the full distance of six rounds, and in the third round, Ray suffers a nasty cut over one eye. Watching him retaliate is almost an act of intimacy; I know what it's like to see his mongoose stare, to feel one of his punches land before I've seen it coming, to be caught off balance by that strange, slithery, sideways move he does, nearly a dance step. When Ray is declared the winner, he looks both relieved and exalted. Hector embraces him warmly, laughing, and rushes off to prepare Arturo.

The two blondes stand and cheer as Arturo makes his entrance. In white satin shorts with ARTURO on one thigh and GATTI on the other, and glittery blue sneakers, he looks small and slight: at five foot eight and 134 pounds, he's almost exactly my size. Possessing an astonishing record of 20–1, with 17 knockouts, this fight brings it up to 18:

91

Arturo's bout lasts less than one round. When his opponent goes down for the count, Arturo races around the ring, leaping onto the supports in each corner and spreading his arms triumphantly for the crowd's cheers. Listed as from Jersey City (although he was born in Canada), the local crowd here takes him as one of their own.

The last fight on the card is for the IBF Junior Lightweight Championship and features Ed Hopson, Lou Duva's fighter. Ed wins, knocking his opponent, Moises Pedroza, out cold for about four minutes in the seventh round. The paramedics revive him, and Pedroza, a Colombian with a 14–0 record that included 13 knockouts, staggers out of the ring, one glove upraised in some sort of victory, perhaps against death. The crowd applauds respectfully.

Backstage, Hector is waiting with Raymond, who wants the cut over his eye stitched up, but the fight doctor hired by Bally's may be more concerned with Pedroza. Hector is pleased that both of his fighters won; he's gloating that Lou Duva won't want his boxer to fight Arturo. "He has no heart!" The guy who laid out his opponent has no heart? "He scared to fight Arturo," says Hector, "so he try to get into another weight class. You see." Arturo is packing up his gear and still looks fresh. "Like movie star!" Hector exclaims, bursting with pride. "Forget about it, eh? Movie star!"

"I think I'm going over to the hospital," Ray says. "I wait there in the emergency room, it's faster. I stay here tonight, and I take the bus home, if I don't find my friends." I'm committed to return to the city with Hector after the fight. Without Ray, I see it's going to be a very long, very awkward two and a half hours.

I'm not wrong. Hector plays salsa music most of the way back and sings along lustily, drumming on the steering wheel. He reaches over occasionally to tousle my hair as I glumly stare out the window at the monotonous landscape of the New Jersey Turnpike. *Please let this trip end.* He gleefully translates some of the lyrics for my behalf; all of them concern a woman loving a man. Shortly before we get to the Holland Tunnel, he brings up the subject of his family, and his plans to buy a house in Brooklyn. "I do it, no' for me, but for them," he says. As his wife and children reside in Panama, I'm not sure how this helps them out exactly, and I don't ask for details. It amazes me that he can put on this family man act after the previous evening's performance. I hope he's decided to forget about the whole unpleasant incident.

When female professional boxer Christy Martin burst on the scene the following year, I knew we had absolutely nothing in common, and that our experiences were entirely different: She married her trainer. Oh, what a luxury that would be, to feel safe with your trainer.

BREAKTHROUGH

IT'S THE MONDAY after our weekend in Atlantic City, the first time we've trained together since we got back. Hector and I are running through some drills before I get in the ring to spar. I'm not wearing my protective headgear or a mouthguard; both are unnecessary when practicing combinations. Hector is gruff and impatient with me, far more than usual.

At one point, my right arm fails to spring back fast enough to protect my side after I throw a punch. Suddenly, Hector pulls back his mitt and hits me, hard, on the right side of my head, catching my ear, my temple, and my cheekbone in one almighty swat. My head jerks to the left.

Tears instantly spring to my eyes from the force of the impact. The pain is incredible, as if a hot needle has been thrust into my inner ear. My temple is throbbing, and my cheek is ablaze. The urge to cry out is like a physical mass in my chest. I gulp hard and blink rapidly, desperate to suck back the tears, anything to stop them from rolling down my face.

Treat me the same way you treat Raymond or Joe or Arturo. That's what I said to him in the hotel room in Atlantic City, and now I'm being punished. Furious at my rejection, he's daring me to quit, and as I stand here and take this abuse, I know something he doesn't: He can knock me out before I'll cry.

For once, it's a relief to get into the ring. My opponent is an eighteen-year-old Hispanic kid named Jesse, so doe-eyed and pretty he looks sixteen. He's sporting the requisite tough-guy accoutrements: a goatee and a tattoo of a tiger on his upper arm. At five foot six, he flaunts the beefed-up arms and upper torso of the short man overly sensitive about his height.

He smirks and looks around as I climb into the ring. "Hello, Tiger," I say, adjusting the position of my mouthpiece with my tongue. A *girl*? He scrutinizes my breasts until the bell rings. We touch gloves, and I lose myself in the aggression of the next three minutes. My rage toward Hector is channeled to this kid; my punches connect solidly.

Jesse, on the other hand, is avoiding any body shots, perhaps out of reverence for my breasts. His punches to my face are only disorienting rather than debilitating.

"Why don't you use your full combination?" he says between rounds. Stunned that he spoke in the ring, I shield him from Hector's view, in case we're commanded into silence. "Like this," he says, pulling up my left arm, crooking my elbow, and aiming my fist to the side of his head. "I was expecting you to do that. You got a good right, you set that up, you need to follow it with something other than a jab. People figure out what you do next."

"Okay," I say, dumbfounded at this invitation. "I'm always nervous to try new things in the ring, you know, things happen so fast, I don't want to do anything but what I know works."

The bell rings again, and I can't help but smile a little as we dance around and throw some jabs. I try the three-pronged attack and miss with all three. He dodges them neatly; of course, he knew what was coming. I throw a right. Another right, then a left to his temple. Like *that*! He takes this opportunity to smash in my exposed side.

"Mother*fuck*er!" I hiss out, as he laughs, drooling a little out of his mouthpiece. His eyes are dancing with smug satisfaction. A big fan of the feint, he uses it so often that I start using it too; start to throw a left, halt suddenly, and then throw a right. A "fake out" seems too elementary to really work, but following your opponent's moves becomes a habit; it's easy to get sloppy and assume that a left hook will continue moving, rather than suddenly stop, making way for a surprise right.

By the end of round two, his repeated blows to the sides of my head are starting to give me a headache. What was it that the guy in Atlantic City said? Headgear protects your looks but not your brain? The bell rings, and we retreat to our corners.

"You do good," Hector says. I glare at him, refusing any pleasure from this unexpected compliment. "Stop pushing! Pull you arm back!" After drinking, I step back into the center of the ring and roll my shoulders. My opponent approaches.

"I had a fight last week," he says. "I lost. I was trying too hard for a knockout, you know? Just watching for that one moment, and he outboxed me on points." He shrugs. "You should hit the body more. All you do are head shots."

"Stan' up!" Hector shouts. I look over in alarm. He's pointing at my crooked stance. I hop gently on both feet until the bell sounds. Knowing it's my last round of sparring for the day, I give my all, surprising the kid once with a hard right to his nose. He snorts in alarm, the panic of worry that the rush of fluid is blood and not mucus. I enjoy this moment, relishing the power: I know how to hit.

In the locker room after the workout, another woman walks in. I've seen her before: short brown hair, mid-thirties, never spars with anyone other than her trainer. Our conversation thus far has been limited to "Hello" and "See you later."

"Hey," I ask, interrupting my search for Advil as she walks past. "Do you ever have a problem with any sexual harassment here? With your trainer?"

"Are you kidding? It's a fact of life," she says. "I switched trainers because of it. I just wasn't interested, and forget it, you know? Now I'm with this other guy, but I don't know, maybe the same thing will happen again."

"Yeah, I'm kind of having those problems right now," I say, lowering my voice. Never know who's next door. "It's making things difficult."

"They didn't want women in the army either. We gotta show them we're not going to go away." I'm cheered a little by this platitude, even though I'm not sure that Gleason's is the right spot to be fighting the good fight for women's equality. Even the men here aren't equal. But at least their trainers aren't trying to have sex with them.

I stop in at Hector's office to pay him for the upcoming week. Whenever there's a lull in training, he can be found in there with Gigo or a couple of other cronies, playing an aggressive and passionate game of dominoes. I'd never seen grown men playing what I considered a child's game, but judging from the crows of triumph and rapid-fire Spanish that occasionally accompany the slapping down of tiles, there's money involved. I step into his office, his world, money in hand.

"Here. See you Wednesday."

Hector looks up and rushes to his feet, squeezing out

from behind his desk. He takes the money and softly grips my hand in a manner that could almost be interpreted as consoling.

"Ho-kay," he says, with a gentleness that I'm tempted to think means he knows he went too far, that he feels badly about his behavior. *Bastard.* I don't gratify him with a smile and instead glance at my watch as if to indicate that I'm running late, pull my hand back, and walk out.

Aside from that brief display of penitence, Hector serves up the same amount of punishment on Wednesday. On Friday, when getting on the train to Brooklyn constitutes an act of bravery in itself, I rehearse a speech for Hector as I walk to the gym: I have to go to Los Angeles on business and won't see him again until the following Friday. It's not at all true, but a break seems imperative if tears are to be prevented. And perhaps he needs a break from me too.

The brief speech delivered, Hector absorbs it with scarcely a nod, and the workout begins with some shadow-boxing while he drills Joe with mitts. Alone, unsupervised, my reflection wobbles in the cheap mirror on the wall, a surface closer to reflective wallpaper than glass.

As I run through some combinations, moving forward, backward, side to side, methodically throwing punches and checking my form, there's a grim woman staring back at me, who looks on the verge of stopping entirely. The seductive thought of simply dropping my arms, unwrapping my hands, and walking out, never to return, is as tempting as climbing into a soft bed after sleeping on nails. *I'll quit. Fuck it. I'll get another goddamned trainer. This is bullshit.*

Hector walks in my direction; now I punch the air with more authority. Watching me for a moment, he explodes. "Move you body!" Several boxers turn in alarm. Who is he addressing like that?

"Don' go like tha'!" he shouts again. "Like thees!" He pounds one foot on the ground.

"What?" I snap back.

"Move you leg!"

Gritting my teeth to stop from crying or screaming in frustration, I shout back, "Do you want me to keep it *here?*" Stamping my foot. "Or *here?*" Shifting it to the side. "What do you *want?* Move it *how? Where?*"

"Move . . . you . . . leg!" The entire gym is holding its collective breath. Even the boxers on the heavy bags behind us are pulling their punches in order to hear every word.

"Hector . . ." I say, my voice as firm and authoritative as possible, but there's a slight wobble on the second syllable. Deep breath. "Can I talk to you in your office, please?" Meaning, *away from this crowd that is listening to our every word.*

"No! We working now!"

"You're making this personal!" I yell back, teeth bared. "I don't think your attitude has been right ever since *Atlantic City.*" The two words hang in the air, daring him to push me to spell it out for all assembled. The bell signaling the start of a round has sounded, but the activity level is still at a minimum. Standing among those at the heavy bags, Joe Gatti is watching, wide-eyed.

Hector speaks slowly, patronizingly. "You wan' me to treat you like a boxer! You see how I am with them!"

"As long as what you're doing is about *BOXING,* and not about *ANYTHING ELSE.*"

"Yes, ees about *boxing!*" He spits the word out as if it tastes bad.

Shaking with rage and frustration, I add, "Because if it's *for any other reason,* tell me now, and I walk right out of here."

Grabbing my head with both hands, Hector suddenly gives me a Bugs Bunny kiss, a huge, wet smacky-sounding kiss that covers the side of my face.

"And no kissing!" I yell, but with less anger and more relief. It was Hector's training that brought both of his boxers victory this past weekend, and I am desperate to stay within this magic circle of skill. I need Hector. "You don't kiss Joe, don't kiss me!"

Hector turns around. "Joe, wha's the firs' thing I do when you win a fight?"

"Kiss me," Joe says with a grin.

"Okay!" I say, pointing at Hector. "After I win a fight, you can kiss me. But not in training."

"Sure!" he says, as if that's been settled long ago.

We resume the workout, and the clamor of Gleason's

rises again to normal levels. Hector works with me on the mitts. The relief now that the air has been publicly cleared has exhausted me, but Hector is gentler, more protective. At the end of the workout, I'm still grateful that I told him earlier that I'd see him in a week. If I had to tell him now, he might think the very worst—that I am a coward.

———

The week passes without a visit to Gleason's, but I still do the running and weight training. Last year, when I was training with my longtime trainer Pat Manocchia for the Marathon, running seemed like such an exhausting, overwhelming, and frightening experience, especially as the mileage went up and up and up. And now, trotting easily with him, through the springtime glory that is Central Park, I wonder what on earth was I so scared of back then. In the Marathon, no opponents are hiding in the bushes waiting to spring out and beat you to a pulp.

"God, what a scaredy-cat I was back then," I muse aloud. "I didn't know how easy I had it."

"Courage is not about the absence of fear," Pat points out, "but the presence of it. It's the ability to act in spite of being afraid."

While it didn't seem profound in the park, it stays with me the rest of the day. Back at home, I write it on a small slip of paper and tape it to my bathroom mirror.

———

"I'm taking a beating here!" This plea is not from me but from David, my opponent, a fortysomething ex–Wall

102

Street man turned rap singer who calls himself the Renegade Jew. The state knows him as an ex-felon who spent
time in jail for tax evasion. As I bit down on my mouthpiece, Hector told me, "He hates to be hit in the nose."

His nose is the only place I'm trying to hit him. He's joking between punches, but I can tell I've hurt him a few
times.

"You remind me of my ex-wife!" he says. This form of
psychological warfare, whether it is intended to make me
laugh or to make me see that we should be united rather
than fighting (we of the same socioeconomic class) offends
me. As the weaker boxer, I know that when I choose to
remind the person I'm fighting that they really shouldn't
hit me so hard, so often, it's a desperate move. But it's
cowardly, unseemly, *unmanly* for a man to plead his case
with me.

My week off has magically bestowed a new power and
force in my punches. My arms race back to position, my
concentration is improved, and my movements are more
instinctual, less clumsy. It's like that galvanizing moment
when you learn a new dance, and you realize you've
stopped counting out the beats and are simply, effortlessly
moving to the music. Hector whistles appreciatively as I
step back out of the ring, then hums a low tone, a small
dirge to the Renegade Jew.

One of the onlookers is Mike Martinez, who once fought
at the Garden. "She hit like an animal!" Hector says to him
with pride.

"You doin' good! A little bay-cation," Hector muses as he unwraps my hands at the end of the workout. "I geev you a break, you use you experience. . . ." He nods, happy with my improvement. As I rise up from my ten push-ups, the final capping-off to a letter-perfect workout, he leans close, laughing a little.

"I wondered when you were gonna blow." He mimics crying, a screwed-up face, sobbing boo-hoo-hoo, the exaggerated gesture of shoulders shaking.

"Who, me?" Incredulous, I wonder who he could be talking about. My one victory here has been that he never saw me cry.

"You!" He cries again, like a sissy. "An' you did!" He laughs and claps me on the back, as if to cheer me up, show me there's no hard feelings. "There a lot of pressure to be a boxer! You see tha' now!"

Let him think what he wants. He never saw me cry.

BROKEN

"HEY, RAY," I call out across the ring. "It's my birth-day." As mine falls in late May, it meant childhood parties on the patio, and sleepovers where jars of lightning bugs glowed next to our sleeping bags. As a teenager, a picnic at the beach was the rule if it fell during the long Memorial Day weekend, a time when everyone feels like cutting loose. My birthday has always felt like the start of sum-mer, like a special holiday, where games should be for-feited, scores rearranged in my favor, seats offered, tabs picked up.

The bell rings, and we touch gloves. Ray's workout gear, black shorts and a maroon T-shirt, are as clean and crisp as his red leather gloves and headgear. His fastidious nature carries through to his boxing, which is always precise and graceful even when he's fast and brutal.

I start the round with a few opening punches, intending them as signals to Ray that I'm still game to box a little, even though it's my birthday and he'll be going easy on me. I throw my usual combination: left, right, uppercut; the first two whiz by his ever-bobbing head, and the last thuds meaninglessly against his forearms. Trotting backward, I watch his face, a suddenly glowering mask of intimidation. He advances toward me in three quick steps, forcing me into a corner. My arms raise defensively in anticipation of a light flurry. "Happy . . ." says Ray, and his arm shoots toward me with a killer punch that smashes hard into my left side.

". . . birthday." The blow that accompanies the brutal salutation connects with my right side.

His first punch delivers a sickening revelation: *My ribs are now pressing dangerously hard against my lung. A major organ is now being squashed like a caterpillar underneath a gardening boot.* A punch against muscles can feel like a cramp, or a stinging lash, or a thudding agony, but it is still distant from the real action of your innards. This punch feels as if it were delivered in an operating room, a horribly wrong slip of the scalpel, the sudden dropping of a clamp into the delicate anemone folds of my guts.

The air leaves my body in one hideous gasp. Ray steps back, smiling, showing the entire front of his white mouthpiece.

"Wait . . ." I croak, doubled over. My forehead is ablaze, my body is cold and clammy; there's a threat of nausea in the back of my throat. Drooling against my mouthpiece, I manage a weak cough, which triggers a thin flare of pain in my left side. My gloved hand raises high in what I pray is the universally recognized signal of surrender.

"What you doin'!" yells Hector. "Fight! Stan' up!" Raymond is directly in front of me, but all I can see is the carefree shuffle of his sleek black Adidas sneakers. His lack of concern is devastating, and his patient time-step is the reason Hector believes that I'm just faking an injury. Inhaling slowly, I somehow summon the energy for a solid blast of power, enough to rise quickly with an uppercut. My glove catches him on the underside of his chin and jerks his head back. Pain momentarily forgotten, I'm both thrilled and appalled: he must have been looking away.

"Oh," says Ray, his dark eyes peering out malevolently between the twin battering rams of his arms, "you want it that way."

Whatever "that way" could possibly be is enough of a threat to spur me into immediate flight. Bolting across the ring, I make my getaway without technically turning my back on him completely, but the front of my body is twisted protectively into what can only be described as a running crouch. Hector must be momentarily distracted in conversation, as I manage this sloppy move without reprimand. Offering your opponent nothing legal to hit is a cowardly escape, but thinking about it now, I can only marvel that I didn't call a time-out. After six months, I had fully absorbed the Zeitgeist of the ring: to be perceived as a coward, even under these outrageous circumstances, is absolutely unacceptable.

Ray advances. Watching him, casting desperately in my mind for a way to save myself from further injury, I go to the thing that has saved me in the past: words. "You like to hit girls, Ray?" I've regained enough air to make talking trash possible; by inhaling tiny sips of oxygen, I can take shallow breaths without wincing. "That makes you feel good, like a real man?" At this point, shame may be my only weapon. Ray's face betrays no remorse, only amused detachment, the interest of a man holding a magnifying glass over an anthill on a sunny day. Moving my left arm away from my ribs at this point is impossible, an act my brain has vetoed. My elbow is frozen to my side.

"This is my day," croons Ray as he throws another jab. I try to dodge this incoming missile, but the punch lands. My nose flattens beneath it, but to my relief, the punch is not as hard as I had anticipated. Is Ray softening up on me? Am I already in so much pain that a jab to my head is merely annoying, like being hit with a cream pie?

Suddenly I hear Hector bellowing at me to fight. Backing away, I keep my right shoulder angled at Ray, to keep him as far away from my left side as possible. I'm changing my stance to fight like a southpaw and try to lead with my right foot to accommodate my new positioning. It's awkward and clumsy, and I stagger around until the bell rings.

"My ribs," I gasp as soon as my mouthpiece is out. "They hurt. He got me. Really hurt." Hector glares.

"You wan' stan' there, fight! Hold you arms up! Don' drop you arms! Bam, bam, bam," he says, flinging his arms out and returning them instantly. Ray is being attended to by Hector's bearish Doppelgänger, Gigo, who is, like Hector, bedecked in nylon pants and a matching jacket; blue and white on Hector, maroon and green on Gigo. Ray is calmly sipping the water that Gigo is pouring from a large green plastic bottle directly into his mouth. As an extra amenity for his boxers, Hector fills several plastic bottles with tap water, then stores them in the fridge in his office. Gigo is mute and watchful, eyeing me as I drink from my own white plastic bottle while Hector rants. The cool water feels good inside my mouth.

"You don' know to throw punches or protect youself," Hector goes on. "You try to do both! You don' do either!" He pops my mouthpiece back in. "Don' stan' there if you don' fight!"

The bell rings. We touch gloves. "Stay away from my left side," I tell him, an appeal to decency that verges on

LYNN SNOWDEN PICKET

pleading. He smiles, satisfied that I've cried uncle. We spend much of the round in pursuit of each other, and aside from one punch to my left breast, when Ray remembers in midthrow that my left side is off-limits and redirects it north, there are no unpleasant surprises. After the final bell, Hector orders me out of the ring.

Arturo is warming up on the jump rope not far from a poster advertising one of his fights: a grainy black-and-white bill featuring an unsmiling young boxer flexing his arm, clenching his fist. In this photo, Arturo's heavily lidded eyes, protruding brow, and lips pressed into a grim, thin line make his face more like Phantom of the Opera than a movie star. Hector points to Arturo, summoning him over. Holding my breath to steady my torso, I bend over cautiously and ever so gingerly hop down out of the ring, wincing as I land. Worry and fear bring on an escalating fantasy of something shaking loose inside my body. A flying particle of rib puncturing my lung, leaking air, paramedics, the hospital, tubes down my throat.

"You suppose to be in good shape!" Hector says. "What you do yesterday?"

"I ran five miles, lifted weights. I run and lift weights every Tuesday and Thursday, plus I run six miles on Saturdays as well." The good shape remark stung, particularly as it was delivered in front of Arturo. "Ray hit me really hard!"

"Yes, Ray hit hard! You should protect youself!"

110

It's not until I pound away at the speed bag that my breathing somewhat returns to normal. *Now I know what it's like to really get hit,* I think, trying to find the tiny dot of optimism in this bleak landscape. But then dread returns. *Maybe that's not as bad as it can get. Maybe that was nothing.* I glance over to see Raymond and Arturo fighting hard, two professionals locking horns. Raymond is taller and heavier, but his mouth is already hanging open as he desperately sucks air to keep up with this little powerhouse, who is running him all over the ring.

Walking toward the locker room, I pass Ray at the heavy bags. The face that terrified me forty-five minutes ago has relaxed, and his handsome smile beams in my direction. Outside the ring, Ray is a pussycat.

"You really got me," I tell him, trying to appear casual and sporting about it, but fishing for some sort of closure: an apology or explanation perhaps.

"I know," he says. "I saw you go back, and I thought, ohhhh. But you say it's your birthday. It's my mother's birthday, and she makes me angry this morning."

"So you were boxing your mother?"

"No!" he says indignantly.

"Did any of my punches hurt?"

"No."

"Were you . . . surprised by any of them?"

He considers this for a moment. "Yes. They surprised me sometimes."

Hector is standing in his doorway, watching us as he chats with a short, fat man, one of the usual spectators here, someone who spends hours watching boxers. I walk over, seeking reassurance. "Hector, am I hitting hard?" I throw a punch in the air as if I'm signing for the deaf, little clues to help his English comprehension.

"Yes."

"You have a good right," says the fat man. "Strong!"

"Do I hit like a man?"

"Yes, like a man!" says Hector. And when he says that, I take it as the highest compliment. So there it was. I wanted to be like a man. As a woman I was vulnerable, and vulnerability led to pain. It's obvious to me now that I had felt so emotionally exposed by my divorce that I was in search of some kind of armor to keep everyone at a distance. And I must say I succeeded.

To my relief, Hector seems amused by my question, rather than annoyed, which is his usual reaction. Perhaps he doesn't want to be rude to me in front of his friend.

"Raymond says I don't hit hard." *Tattletale.*

"Raymond not gonna tell you," Hector says with a snort of derision. "Raymond hit like an animal."

Emboldened, I walk back to Ray, who is now shadow-boxing in the mirror.

"You know, Ray, you're full of shit. Hector says I hit hard now. He told me I hit 'like a man.' "

"You hit hard, I'll hit you hard. So if you get beaten up"—he stops punching the air and straightens his arms up into a long stretch, like a jungle cat—"it's because you're doing good."

In spite of, and perhaps because of, my ribs, I smile.

———

At home I sit with an ice pack pressed against my side, and a copy of *The Merck Manual of Diagnosis and Therapy* in my lap. There's nothing here that will tell me whether I need to visit the emergency room or take 600 mg. of ibuprofen. An emergency medicine Web site yields seven pages of information on fractured ribs, including the fact that 12 percent of patients with rib fractures die, 94 percent have associated injuries, and 32 percent have hemo- or pneumothoraxes. Other alarming facts swim into view; that a break in a rib has only a 50 percent likelihood of being visible on an X ray, and that something with the name *atelectasis* is a possible complication from such an injury. I reach for the dictionary and see that this condition could have been described in plain English as "total or partial collapse of the lung."

Lungs are peculiar, delicate things. If a rib has torn your lung, the resulting hole becomes a one-way valve. Air leaks out into the chest cavity, but it can't go back in. As there's no way for the air to exit or to be exhaled, it begins to displace the area occupied by the lung, and soon the lung flattens out and collapses. If you stop inhaling deeply, because your ribs are broken and it hurts to do so, the unused section of lung will shrivel and fold in upon itself, adding the likelihood of pneumonia.

The suggested follow-up care to the "adequate analgesic medications" for cracked ribs suggests that the patient be reminded to take deep breaths. Turning off the computer, I inhale slowly. There, that's not too bad; better to risk pain and hyperventilation than lung collapse. My diagnosis: a three-Advil kind of injury.

Running in the park, however, is beyond what ibuprofen can accommodate. The muscles in my chest have clenched around my rib cage like a tight, protective band, and my breathing is uneven and ragged. Slowing down the pace, I ease into ever-deeper breaths, a gradual compromise between what is comfortable and what is advisable if I'm to get enough air to prevent myself from blacking out on the pavement. Two miles pass before I can breathe without surprising my tender ribs. But an unexpected sneeze, brought on by a passing car, feels like a pair of pliers has roughly tugged at the sensitive nerves in my chest.

During the next two weeks, I deliberately show up in the afternoons, pleading a busy morning schedule, and praying for an empty gym and the respite from sparring. With a few exceptions, I get my wish, and my ribs slowly heal.

At home, however, I awaken in the middle of the night, panting for air: a dream that someone is trying to suffocate me.

BLISTERED

THE BIG TOENAIL on my left foot is a sickly green gray. Pressing down on it gingerly, the green mutates in spots to a pale, waxy yellow. Sitting cross-legged on the grubby locker-room carpet, I peer at its variegated surface and wedge a fingernail tip underneath the top edge. Applying gentle pressure upward, my stomach roils a bit as the nail lifts up and pulls halfway off, like the creaking trapdoor to a forbidden basement. I press it back down, as if it could be reattached to the nail bed this way, like a sticker that's been mistakenly peeled off at one corner.

Popping the lid off my well-used jar of Vaseline, I dip my fingers in and coat the toe, the nail, and the heavy ridge of calluses that have built up on the edge of the ball of that foot, stretching up alongside my big toe like a little mountain range. In boxing, my left foot leads, and the calluses are proof of its extra burden, for supporting more weight more often, for bearing the brunt of every quick stop. My right foot, however, is also heavily worn on the inside of the big toe, and there's a tender spot in the center of the ball, from the bracing, the shoving, the leaning into a punch.

This Vaseline ritual is one I started during Marathon training and is common for distance runners; goo is slathered between toes or anywhere there is extra pressure, to prevent chafing and blisters from the friction and heat that will build up inside socks. Runners, like dancers, tend to have calluses on each knuckle and joint, the contact points between feet and shoes, and there is debate, sometimes based on personal preference, as to whether they should be filed down or allowed to grow and build. I still cling to the idea, if not the reality, of pretty feet, so I file my calluses down.

Boxers' feet toughen around the perimeter rather than on the top, from the constant starts and stops, the jamming of one step forward or halting sideways. "Turf toe" is what football players call it: a toenail can only absorb so many headlong collisions with the tip of a shoe before it gives up altogether. The skin on the bottom of my feet has been brutalized as well. It's blistered up twice already from these decelerations, peeling away in large sections off the ball, like fabric torn off a sofa than has been dragged behind a car. The new skin beneath, a bright tomato red, gets Vaselined before being covered by a giant Band-Aid. A bandage will peel off during the workout in much the same way as the skin did, but it seems cruel not to put something extra there before easing my sock over such vulnerable flesh.

I already know the fate of my toenail; I lost this same one nearly a year ago while training for the Marathon, and I was traumatized. Running can cause feet to spread, and mine had forever outgrown my size eight sneakers when this nail turned black. I wasn't terribly concerned, as dark red polish neatly covered this injury, but one morning in the shower, the nail drifted away from my foot toward the drain, where it slowly revolved, a chip of Revlon Vixen amid the soapsuds.

"So what?" was Pat's comment to my choked, traumatized confession of mutilation. But here, pulling on my shoes in Gleason's locker room, the prospect of a lost toenail is nothing at all.

———

Hector watches me shadowbox and fusses at me. "Fast! Bap bap bap!" He's rushing my warm-up so he can put me in the ring with Arturo, like a baby-sitter eager to corral his charges. I step under the ropes with a slight, familiar, low-grade ringing in my ears, the adrenaline of the fight-or-flight instinct kicking in. Arturo says a quick hello between gulps

117

of water. I smile back, nodding, grateful for the pleasantry. Hector grabs the orange case for my mouthguard and squirts water on the molded plastic before shoving it between my lips, shouting instructions to Arturo in Spanish. After waving his arm in a gesture of urgency, he slaps me on the shoulder, as if to prod me forward, buck me up. I bite down on the mouthguard, making sure it's in position around my molars. Inhaling deeply, a tiny glob of saliva hits the back of my throat, causing a minor coughing fit.

The bell rings, and we touch gloves. With arms clamped to his sides, Arturo takes off sideways, and I dutifully follow, jabbing twice, missing twice. Now he hops laterally in the other direction, and I switch gears, feeling the Band-Aid adhesive shift on my left foot and give way. More jabs. More misses. He yanks his head backward, sideways, enjoying my frustration. His lips are clamped shut, but his eyes are smiling, sparkling. He crosses to the side, to the corner, across the ring, dancing around easily. I follow as if I'm trying to guard him in a game of one-on-one basketball. I hear my breathing: it's regular and controlled, as if I'm running. He throws a body blow and catches me in my left shoulder, so fast I don't see it until I feel it, stopping my jab in midthrow. I crash a right into his forearms. And that's when he swings the left into my temple.

The moment after such an impact is painless and infinite, a world-scalding clarity that people must search for in religion and drugs, and here it is, mine, the mystical payoff for being clocked in the skull by Arturo "Thunder" Gatti.

Every detail of the room opens up in one glaring instant, every molecule is laid bare, time slows to a crawl. I see a tiny piece of lint hang precariously, absurdly, to a lock of shiny black hair that's peeking out of Arturo's headgear. I want to reach up and gently pull it away. A whooshing sound floods into my ears. Arturo backs off. The world catches up.

Hector is shouting for me to fight. I stumble toward Arturo and throw an uppercut that he bats down—with a fierce hammer blow to my forearm. I swing my torso away and drop that arm, shielding it with my body.

"Put you hands up!" Hector yells, appalled. I raise them but maintain my distance. Arturo bobs in place, head down, like a bull warming to the charge. I advance but move to the left, buying time, when to my relief, he backs off again and I'm able to at least pretend that I would hit him, if only I could catch him. The bell rings, and I limp over to Hector, the sole of my left foot ablaze.

He holds the ropes up for me to exit, and my heart leaps at the reprieve, but he's already pointing at the next ring, where a sinewy, strung-out guy in his early thirties in duct-taped headgear is furiously shadowboxing: my next sparring partner. I hop down and look back at Arturo. His attention is fixed on his next opponent, a sleek, heavy-browed Hispanic guy with shoulders that look carved out of stone. Arturo glances over, feeling my stare.

"You were good," he calls out, his speech slightly thicker through a mouthguard. "No one can keep up with me! You're the first. You're a runner! In good shape." I smile and look at Hector.

"Hey, what do you think about that?" I say, greedy for water. Hector glares his answer back.

"Two round," he says, pointing again to the next ring.

The difference between fighting a professional and fighting a practiced amateur is in the precision of the blows. The professional fighter's punches land before you see them coming. A practiced amateur swings wildly, an extravagance of energy out of proportion to the payoff. With the nonprofessional, you might have the luxury of seeing a punch coming, but the punishment for staying in its path is likely to be severe. Guys who box as a hobby probably came into the sport because they were either naturally good at it, or they enjoyed pummeling people, or both. The ones to fear are brawlers and street fighters, their hands securely connected to, and controlled by, their ego.

"Dominick!" he says by way of introduction. He seems a little wired, a little frantic for someone who's been shadow-boxing all alone. He seems too old to be entertaining ideas of turning pro but he's training too hard for someone who's just here for a workout. There's a strange, glittery excitement to his eyes.

"Lynn."

"Linda?" He smiles, showing a black mouthguard, and I nod. Most people in Gleason's assume my name is short for Linda, and I'm tired of correcting them.

"Oh, *sí! Lin*da!"

"Okay, here we go," says Dominick, as we touch gloves. I back up immediately, recalling Hector's advice. "Nice and easy," he told me a week ago, when I got in the ring with a heavyweight. "Don' go up to them swingin' right away, or they get scared, hit you back."

A light jab to his shoulder. Another to his forearm. Dominick throws a wild roundhouse that careens in from my left; it's blocked by my forearm. He uses the other fist to sneak in a poke to my ribs. I moan softly, deliberately, even though it didn't hurt very much. If he's getting off on the thought of hurting me, I want him to think he has. Hector, meanwhile, has been notably silent.

There's good reason for my caution: Dominick carries the tension of a lit fuse. Hunched forward, his forearms are tightly clasped to his chest, his head is down, while his feet shuffle stiffly about. Suddenly he shoots off a flurry of blows. I block most, but a left hook catches me in the jaw. There's a pranging sound inside my mouth. I must reset my mouthpiece, wincing a little. He smiles: a wedge of blackness. The bell rings.

Walking over to my corner, I see the reason for Hector's silence: he's been watching Arturo. Now he turns back to me. I open my mouth for a drink, and Hector pulls out my mouthpiece. A long trail of bloody drool follows. My eyes widen, and after swallowing, my tongue goes on an exploratory mission for an open cut. Maybe something on the gum line in the back.

"Keep you hands up," Hector admonishes. "Bring them

back fast! Why you leave them out?" Nodding and swallowing, I take the abuse and advice. Boxers aren't supposed to explain or defend choices between rounds: it's too
exhausting and only angers your trainer. The bell rings
again. We touch gloves.

Dominick is either more relaxed in the second round, or
just tired. His movements are slower, and I'm able to practice more of my offensive moves without the worry of scar-
ing him into full retaliation. One, two, three—my uppercut
misses wildly, and suddenly he locks his arm through mine
and pulls me in for a clinch. It's a wrestling move. He has
my arm pinned around him, my head is straining against his,
and the duct tape on his headgear is pressing against my
cheek. As we grapple, I strain against him, and with every
inhalation, I smell his scalp, an unwanted, revolting side-
bar of motor oil, old carpeting, cold Chinese take-out.

"Hey!" Hector yells. Before he can go on, Dominick has
released me. "What you doing!" I turn to look at Hector, to
shoot a reproachful look. "Look where you fighting!"

Furious, I fire off a hard right, and it lands solidly into
his face. He charges at me, all body blows. I curl up and
keep my arms solid. After taking three or four, panic takes
over, and I rush sideways, deciding to push the contest to
my advantage by making it an endurance event. I let him
chase me the rest of the round.

At the end of my workout, when I'm jumping rope,
Dominick is walking out, bag in hand. He stops in front of
me and smiles. "You show me respect, I like that. Most

girls don't show any respect. You show respect, it's a good thing." I nod warily, bewildered. A dirty fighter who professes to value *respect* in the ring? If I have to spar with this nutcase again, I'll make sure that Hector keeps an eye on him.

————

Walking up the hill toward the subway station, I realize I can't close my jaw. With a great deal of effort and some pain, I can make my molars meet, but just barely. It's almost as if there's an invisible rod in my mouth. How will I eat?

Half an hour later, I'm sitting in the examining room in my doctor's office, my gym bag on the floor near my feet.

"I think my jaw's dislocated. It was a hard punch, but I didn't feel anything unusual at the time. I'm not sure if I could close my mouth then or not. I was wearing a mouthguard, but I try not to clench my teeth together when I fight." Oddly enough, Dr. Goldberg isn't paying the least bit of attention to my jaw. He's spraying my shoulders and neck with something icy cold.

Placing his hands on my shoulders, he presses down, gently at first, then with some force. "Feel better?" he says.

The thick cord of tension running the length of my neck has been magically cut.

"Close your mouth. How does it feel?"

"I can close it! It feels fine!" I press my molars together again. The rod is gone. "What happened?"

"There's a nerve that runs up here," he says, tracing a path along my neck to my throat, ending at my jaw. "You're so tense, the pressure in your shoulders was pinching it." He rubs my shoulders roughly. "Relax! Get a massage!"

I feel ridiculously foolish. Dislocated jaw, indeed.

"Seriously," he says as I pick up my bag. "Learn to relax, okay?"

THE BOYFRIEND

MY EFFORTS AT relaxing were limited entirely to drinking heavily in East Village bars with Eli and running in the park with my friends. In addition to this truncated routine, I would see my ex-husband once a month for dinner. I hoped that talking to him would provide some sort of closure, but it served only to keep the wounds raw. For days after I would obsess over his every word and wonder why my many questions about our relationship were never answered: *Why did you think I would never find out about the other woman in your life? Did you think I wouldn't hear her messages on the answering machine? How often did you need to go off on a long weekend "by yourself to think"?* I was disgusted with him and furious with myself. And I would take this fury with me everywhere, but particularly into the ring.

————

Vidal Rodriguez is my sparring partner for the day; his name is written in silver Magic Marker across his headgear. Vidal easily clears six feet in height but is lanky with thin limbs. He has the build of a lightweight but not the lightning-fast speed. He lumbers around the ring like a heavyweight past his prime. His only advantage is in having a longer reach than the other boxers in his weight class.

We've just boxed a pleasurable three rounds: Vidal never hit me in the face, and while he was primarily practicing his defense, he was shockingly slow about it, and easy to tag. No racing around, no brutal punches. Just three rounds of hitting a human heavy bag.

When we climbed into the ring together and touched gloves, he said, "I have a seventeen-two record." This bald fact would have terrified me if I hadn't been looking at his nose, which had been broken and rebroken and broken again, by the looks of it, every time he boxed. It was entirely flat from the bridge to the tip, and the cartilage that once gave it depth was shifted over to the right at the top. Then at the flared, flattened nostrils, it curved back to the left. This was not the Brando style of broken nose, where a flaw renders it more perfect. This was like the nose on a clay bust that was accidentally dropped face first before being pushed into the kiln.

When we finish sparring, I ask him if he ever feels fear in the ring. I'm curious to see if his smashed nose speaks of an indifference to pain, or a respect for it. He blinks twice before speaking.

"You live in Manhattan?"

"Yeah," I say. As usual, the word *fear* among boxers is treated as an embarrassment: the only polite, civilized response is to ignore it entirely.

"Live alone?"

"Are you asking me if I have a husband or a boyfriend?"

"Yeah."

"Yes, I do."

He shrugs. "Okay, baby."

"I have a boyfriend." Repetition for added emphasis and also for annoyance that he directed questions to discover that answer, while I was trying to have something of a real conversation.

He addresses me as "baby" for the rest of the afternoon. Each time we pass each other, it's "Hello, baby," "Doin' good, baby," or "Hey, baby." I largely ignore the comments, glaring once with slightly raised eyebrows, but it gets under my skin. It's not the word so much as the loose, superior way he uses it. It also makes me think of another boxer I've seen training here, a hulking black heavyweight who's always with a middle-aged, paunchy white man, either his trainer or his manager. If he's a trainer, he's not very good—he just stands and watches; as a manager, he'd be better off on the phone arranging bouts than just hanging around.

On one occasion, this boxer was pounding a heavy bag in front of a crowd of "interested parties": potential investors who might want to invest in him now and take a chunk of his winnings later. One man held an unlit cigar at his side while he repeatedly checked a beeper on his belt; the other three stood with arms folded across rumpled suit jackets. If posted near a courtroom, they might be cut-rate, ambulance-chasing lawyers. These men were looking at this boxer with some skepticism while his manager/trainer/handler urged his charge to perform. The boxer is a giant, a brutish monster, a man who you would never in a million years instinctively call "baby." And yet as he let loose on the heavy bag, this handler was shouting, *"Go* on, baby!" "Yeah, baby!" and *"Come* on, baby!" to spur him on to reveal even more bankable abilities. It took me a few seconds to figure out why the epithet sounded so disturbing and out of place: it was as if the handler were at a racetrack, yelling at a horse he had bet on, and a crowd of onlookers were there appraising the animal, pound for pound. When Vidal called me baby, it implied intimacy, but this guy said "baby" without affection, as if he owned him.

———

"Hector, where's my mouthguard?" I'm standing in the doorway of his office. He's alone at his desk, eating rice and beans out of an aluminum take-out container, using a plastic fork. A stack of neatly folded paper napkins rests next to the phone. "Do you have it?"

"Where you mouthguar'?"

"I think I left it out here two days ago. It's not in my locker. Maybe I didn't take it into the locker room after I sparred last time. I thought maybe you had it."

"I don' have. Where you leave it?"

Clearly Hector will be no help, so I walk out without another word to look around the gym myself, maybe ask Bruce if there's a lost and found. Passing Hector's equipment locker, a flash of orange peeks out from the top of the cabinet. Success! I reach up and grab it and pop open the bright little case. It's empty. Flipping the case over, as if the clear plastic mouthguard might, absurdly, be stuck to the bottom, I keep turning it and shaking it, unwilling to fully comprehend what has happened. When my mouthguard is not in my mouth, it's in the case. Could it be that someone has actually *taken* my mouthguard? The empty case means someone wanted a piece of plastic that's an exact impression of my mouth, something I've bitten, drooled, and bled on. This is far creepier and more intimate than discovering someone has taken your underwear out of the washing machine at the Laundromat.

Still holding the case, I scan the gym. Two wrestlers are bellowing at each other in the far ring, methodically slamming each other into the canvas. Two big guys are working the heavy bags. Three other boxers are clustered at the

129

mirrors; a few are working speed bags. Jesse, the young boxer with the tiger tattooed on his biceps, is walking in with a young girl hanging on his arm, trailing a cluster of friends. Hardly anyone looks in my direction, mostly because everyone is trying to sneak glances at the small film crew here interviewing Mitch "Blood" Green.

Green, the boxer most famous for losing a sidewalk brawl with Mike Tyson, is wearing his usual bright green satin. Today it is in the form of a heavy quilted jacket and matching pants. The jacket is unzipped slightly to reveal ropes of gold chains, which offset the jacket's ornate gold and red embroidery of his name, which is positioned over his heart; the design is repeated on the back of his jacket in a giant circular logo. His hair is meticulously set in tiny corkscrews that glisten like wet vines creeping down onto his forehead and temples. Gold glasses rest on his crooked nose, one lens sporting his initials in press-on gold letters. He's sitting on a stool near the ring closest to the door, and an interviewer is perched on a stool opposite. The cameraman is fussing with a light on a tripod, and Mitch takes the opportunity to carefully dab at his forehead with a large white handkerchief. Three gold rings sparkle in the morning sun which streams through the coal-dust grime of the windows.

Walking into Bruce's office, I wave the little orange case and ask him if there's a lost-and-found area.

"What did you lose?" he says, raising his eyes from the small screen of his laptop computer.

"My mouthguard. It's always in this case. I found the case, but it's gone."

"I have a lost and found, but that isn't in it." He looks at a young kid sitting in one of the chairs. "Have you seen it around?" The kid shakes his head. "I tell people not to leave things out, as they disappear."

"But who would take a mouthguard? That's so—personal! It's like a toothbrush!"

"You'd be surprised what people take."

If Bruce were a police officer, I'd tell him this wasn't petty theft, it's more of a sex crime, some sort of perversion. Unbidden, the image of a hulking, tattooed, ex-con enters my mind, licking my mouthguard with a long, snakelike tongue.

Minutes later, after purchasing a new yellow mouthguard, I'm standing in Hector's office while he boils the water. After biting down hard on the mouthguard and holding it in place for a minute, I trim the ends down with a pair of scissors, so they don't poke into my gums.

"Come on, let's go!" Hector says, impatient with my fussing. I hand over the case with its new yellow treasure and take a jump rope.

The incident with my mouthguard has brought my usual simmering anger much closer to the surface. It doesn't help that I hear Jesse say to Hector, "With *her*? Oh, man!" Jesse is glistening with a layer of sweat, and his hairless torso reveals every sinew and muscle, the skin taut and rippling. He's been going through an energetic warm-up of jumping rope and shadowboxing as a show for his girlfriend and her friends, all of whom are flustered and giggling, nudging one another. There are a couple of boys in the group, who are more somber and cowed. The girlfriend is wearing tight red pants and a white blouse tied underneath her breasts. Her hair is braided and fastened by red barrettes, which match the glossy red of her lipstick. She periodically covers her eyes when she looks at him, perhaps embarrassed by his blatant promise of raw sexual aggression and power.

I climb into the ring, and Hector fastens my headgear and pops in the new mouthpiece. Chewing on it to get rid of some stiffness, I watch my opponent as he talks a little to his friends sitting near the ring. He's clearly upset that on this day, with a crowd watching, he has to fight a girl. Now he's looking down, shaking his head, rolling his shoulders.

"Hey!" I call out to him, an attempt to remind him that I'm a human being, and that it's possible for us to enjoy the workout together, and to stop being an asshole about what is, in his opinion, an unfortunate turn of events. "We meet again! Are these your friends?"

The bell rings. We touch gloves. I back up and tap him a few times, taking Hector's advice to start slow, but he advances quickly toward me, and we simultaneously deliver body blows. Easily taking my punch, he quickly swings a wild right hook and clocks me in the jaw. What follows is a series of punishing jabs and uppercuts that I'm desperate to repel. My arms slide weakly away as his fists land wherever he wishes. I can hear Hector yelling at me to "Move!"

and I do, but in an effort to move out of what feels like a hail of bullets, I make the fatal mistake of moving my left foot first across my right, which dangerously narrows my base. Tiger Man lands a punch to my left side as I take this blundering step, and the momentum is complete. I hit the canvas in two stages: my right hip, then a second later, my right shoulder. As I fall, I hear the high-pitched squeal of a woman's voice, and I pray it isn't mine.

It isn't. It's the girlfriend. As I fall, my legs are indelicately splayed in the air for a moment, and while I would dearly love to lie flat out and just rest for the duration of the round, I'm also utterly humiliated. I look up and see Jesse laughing. His friends have leaped to their feet and are clustered against the ropes, peering in at me. Their eager, excited faces say: *Is she out cold? Is there blood?*

"Damn it," I mutter as I spring to my feet, furious about the laughing, which qualifies as insult more damaging than injury. After all of the punches I've sustained, it's this one, in combination with my own boneheaded misstep, that finally puts me down: a move similar to the jokester sticking his foot out and tripping a passerby. I'm not dazed as much as embarrassed. "Looking good for your girl, huh?" I rasp when we shuffle around each other again, arms raised. "Afraid I'll put you down with a lucky punch and she won't go out with you anymore?"

I swing wildly at him and miss, which is more exhausting than if the punch lands. I try a hard right, remembering this kid once complimented me on it when we sparred before. It connects, he jerks backward. I follow, exhaling hard. Body shots. He shields himself expertly and throws a quick jab that snaps my head to the right. Disoriented for a second, I back up, buying time to shake the fuzz out of my vision. Advancing, I launch a flurry of uppercuts and body blows and hear a voice yelling "You gotta hit harder than that! You gotta hit harder than that!"

One of his friends telling him to hit me harder? I back up again and move around to the side. He throws a punch, and we lock into a clinch. I flail weakly at his ribs with my left hand, but he's gripping me tightly. That he can do this without reprimand means Hector has either walked away from the ring or is momentarily distracted, deep in conversation. I can feel hot breath on my neck, moist and sticky. "Are we dancing now?" I ask him, my speech slightly slurred from the mouthpiece, which still feels foreign. He slugs hard into my kidney, an illegal punch, pushes me away, then smacks a glove flatly to the side of my head, like a cat lashing out with a paw. This gives him an idea: he claps both gloves up to my ears. My head rings like it was gonged, as I contemplate how I've just had my ears boxed in a boxing ring: how perfectly apt, and how perfectly illegal. He's hitting with a fury that means he's taking no chances: he'd rather be seen as a man beating the crap out of a woman than endure the potential embarrassment of going easy on me, only to get knocked out in front of his friends. I should be flattered that he views me as such a threat, but it's difficult to feel grateful under the circumstances. My left ear is droning like there's a house-fly trapped inside it.

"You gotta hit harder than that! You wanna be in the Golden Gloves, baby, you gotta hit harder than that!" I risk a sideways glance and see that Mr. Green has wandered over to our ring and is now grandly dispensing advice for the benefit of the crew, which is now packing up. "Baby, you better hit harder than that!" he bellows at me, as I slug out a few weak punches. "Harder than *that!*"

Now I'm sick and tired, exhausted *and* fuming. The humiliation of lying prone on the canvas was a bad start, and fighting a guy who's not content to spar but thinks he's fighting for some championship belt has me mad and scared. Hector is less than attentive, which is why my left kidney is throbbing, and on top of that, of all the boxers that this posturing, preening has-been could shout advice to in this entire gym, he picks me. Am I the only one in here who wouldn't try to shove his advice where it belongs? Or is he embarrassing me *because he can?* I raise one glove to Jesse, signaling a brief time-out, and stomp over to the ropes, fists upraised, ready to smash Mitch "Blood" Green's smug, overbearing face in. I pull my right hand back, nostrils flaring to suck in as much air as I can, preparing to exhale with all of the might I can muster, ready to let my fist fly squarely into the bridge of his nose.

And with my arm cocked back, I freeze. Mitch hasn't moved so much as an eyelash. I'm close enough to see that the corner of the initial M is starting to peel away from his glasses, the lenses gazing back at me as unfeeling and in-scrutable as twin television screens. *Am I out of my fucking mind?* I pull my fist back to my side as I exhale noisily, a wordless burr of rage and frustration, and turn back to my opponent. Jesse easily lands one shot high on my chest just before the bell rings; his tiger tattoo advances and retreats in a blur. I limp off, shaking.

Hector appears in my corner. "Make that jerk go away," I tell him, before he starts in on me about falling down. "He's distracting me." Sweating with panic, I'm trying to convince myself that I held my fist up to Green as a warn-ing, perhaps even a playful warning, for him to shut his trap. But what really happened is that I chickened out: I was expecting him to back away, to cry out in mock fear at my bravery, or my arrogance, maybe even to laugh at me. But I looked into the face of that monster and saw that he was poised and *ready*. He was *dying* for me to hit him in the face. And then his hands would have shot through the ropes of the ring and flown around my throat like twin pythons.

Hector's face opens into shock and consternation, as he believes I'm discussing the ejection of my opponent. "*What?* Two more rounds!" he says, as if to a petulant child who refuses to eat his vegetables. He's rinsing my mouthpiece with water.

"No, not him! *Him!* Mitch! He's talking to me!" Mr. Green, however, in the lull between rounds, has wandered off again to chat with the crew and is now shaking hands with one of them as they prepare to take their leave. Hector shoves my mouthpiece in, and the bell rings.

I fight the next two rounds with the calmness that follows the adrenaline rush of a narrowly escaped disaster. Anger has also left Jesse. Perhaps his brief rest gave him the perspective to see that I'm not enough of an opponent to merit such aggression. Numbly going through the motions, I can smell the funkiness of my sweat. Nothing this kid could do right now could scare me more than my own bravado, or stupidity, or whatever it was that led me, shaking with rage, to the edge of the ring.

Later, as I work the speed bag, Hector walks over to study my form. Concentrating on the sound and rhythm of the bag, I pound away at it, controlling its movements with a precision I couldn't have imagined four months ago. The round bell ends, and I slam my wrapped fist into the bag as its final punishment. As it swings wildly in the growing silence, Hector reaches out and touches my upper back, near my shoulder. I'm pouring sweat in this nearly airless room, despite the fact that I'm just in shorts and a black Jogbra with a black tank top over it. The racer-cut style of the tops means a lot of flesh is exposed on my shoulders.

"Thees is a good spot for tattoo," he says, lightly tracing a pattern with his fingertips, a smile curling around his lips. "One that says 'Hector.'"

————

"Hello, my name is Gilbert."

Hector, in his preferred introductory style, has gestured

at this man, who fills in the pertinent information himself. Gilbert, it turns out, is Hector's grown nephew, an attractive, mustachioed, well-spoken man in his early twenties who is visiting from Florida. He doesn't look muscular enough to box, but he seems fairly slim and fit in his jeans and T-shirt that says I SURVIVED HURRICANE ANDREW.

Gilbert says he will be in New York at least through the summer, which is excellent news. Perhaps he can serve as translator when Hector's English fails him in one of our many disagreements. And today I have my own introduction to make.

My boyfriend Eli has come to Gleason's today.

Eli shakes Gilbert's hand, then turns to Hector. "I've heard a *lot* about you," he says. A touch of sarcasm has crept into his voice, indiscernible to all but me.

Suddenly I see Eli through Gleason's collective eyes: he looks boyish and decidedly frail. Despite being twenty-three years old, he looks like he could be the paperboy who's come collecting for the *Evening Post*. He could pass for my kid brother, a nephew, or God help me, my son. With a fourteen-year age difference, it is, I suppose, humanly possible. Eli is what a therapist might call a "nonthreatening" male. And while that's all I wanted in a boyfriend, at Gleason's it means he's weak.

His official purpose here today is to videotape my sparring, so I can see my progress and mistakes with a more objective eye, but we're both aware that one reason I asked him to be here was so I could show off for him: the tough girl in action. For months now, he's heard stories about what I do in this place. It affects our life as a couple. The issue of whether I'll be sparring the next day influences my choice to have more than one glass of wine, to honor my eleven o'clock bedtime, or to see him at all. Eli has, on more than one occasion, seen me popping Advils and asking waiters for a bowl of ice at restaurants so I can tuck several cubes into a linen napkin, to wrap my aching and bruised hands before the food arrives.

The unofficial purpose of Eli's visit is to lend some real meaning to the phrase "my boyfriend," to show everyone here that he does exist. I've asked Eli to remain a respectful distance away while filming to keep interference and distraction to a minimum. As usual, he complies perfectly, occasionally backing away to a wall while I rest. Carefully rationing my eye contact with him, I don't want Hector to yell at me for being less than focused, and I don't want to be seen by other boxers as doing something as undignified as performing for a boyfriend's video camera.

After my workout, when I emerge from the locker room, I see Eli is surrounded by a gang of men. Quickening my stride, I hold my gym bag close to me as I rush across the room to see—or protect him from?—what's going on.

"No, I don't box," Eli is telling Gigo as I breathlessly arrive and break into the circle. "It's not my thing." Gilbert, Dominick, Raymond, Hector, and a few boxers who I've never fought or spoken to before are hanging on his every word. Everyone is smiling like sharks.

"What are you going to do," says one huge boxer wearing a T-shirt bearing the word BOMB on it, "if someone comes up to you on the street and starts messing with your woman?"

Eli bursts out laughing. Later on, he says his laughter was due to the absurdity of such a scenario, and the apparent naïveté of the boxer's idea that we live in a world where evil intentions can be defused with simple boxing skills: "Who gets involved in hand-to-hand conflicts?" he argued that night over dinner. "Some guy 'messes with us,' he'll have a knife, or a gun! What, we're going to fight right there on the street, 'put up our dukes' like we're in *West Side Story* or something? If someone 'messes with me,' it would be better if I had a gun, right?" But at that moment, to the group assembled, he fails to elaborate.

After his short burst of incredulous laughter, Eli gives me an appreciative glance and says admiringly, "I figure she can take care of herself!" The group explodes with laughter, laughing with the manic energy of Western villains when the greenhorn hero announces he's never fired a pistol. "Take care of herself!" Dominick nods incredulously and slaps another boxer on the back.

"What," I ask the group indignantly. "You don't think I can take care of myself?" I shove Raymond, who is still giggling. I pretend to take their laughter as an affront to my abilities, but I know what they're really laughing at.

Here stands my boyfriend, with his backward-facing baseball cap, his torso swimming inside his oversized

T-shirt and baggy button-down shirt, his jeans hanging off his hips. His shoulders, I notice with some discomfort, are not much broader than my own. I had completely misjudged the effect that Eli's presence at Gleason's would have. While Eli correctly assumed that his simple statement was exactly the right feminist-approved response, those eight little words went through the gym like an air raid siren: *There will be absolutely no consequences from this guy, or from anyone else, if we mess with his woman.*

BEATEN

ON THE WALK down the long hill to Gleason's, a man quickly crosses the street toward me. My radar has picked him up as a full-on threat, and my peripheral vision registers he's now behind me and picking up speed. My heart rate rises, and I grip my bag tightly; I don't want to drop it if I have to run. Yet something about him makes me pause in the default decision to cross the street, so I angle my head slightly for a better view, for more clues, and then I see it: the gym bag hanging from one muscled shoulder.

He's a boxer. We're both going to Gleason's. I probably know him.

"Hello!" he says, after I turn around and meet his eyes. My heart rate slows to normal. I've seen him at the gym, but we've neither sparred nor spoken. He's a middleweight with a broad, flat face, tiny eyes and big cheekbones, a small nose and a large chin; his face seems armored, offering nothing but hard surfaces. We exchange pleasantries as he catches up to me. He tells me his name is Godfrey.

"Why do you box?" he says. He's Hispanic, and there's a slight accent to his words.

"Why do you?"

"Because it's my job. I wouldn't do it if I didn't have to."

"You don't enjoy it?"

"If I could do something else, I would! You can do something else!"

"So can you."

He speaks slowly, dragging out the words as if to a slow child. "Why . . . do you . . . want . . . to box?"

"I want to see what it's like. Learn how to hit people. To fight." I can't help but flash back to Eli's observation that boxing skills are hardly the determining factor in establishing dominance on the street. The barrel of a gun would make my right hook a moot point. I have the sinking feeling that while you can teach a rabbit to stand and fight, when faced with a wolf, he's still just a rabbit.

"But you're going to ruin your looks. For me, that's not

important. But for you, you're pretty. If I were a woman, I wouldn't box."

"I have on headgear. That protects me."

"You don't have to do it!" He's not smiling. I'm mildly surprised at his passion; my boxing offends him on some level.

"It's just temporary," I reassure him as we approach the building. First I had to reassure my parents, then friends, then strangers—and now boxers? He shakes his head angrily as we climb the stairs and disappears into the men's room without a backward glance.

Gilbert greets me with a big smile. "Hector's not here. He's in Europe with two fighters." My mouth drops open in exasperation. I wish Hector had had the courtesy to tell me himself. "It's okay," Gilbert tells me. "I'll take care of you."

After changing in the locker room, I emerge, carrying my gear. "Hey! Hey, you!" It's Dominick. His hair has either grown a bit, or maybe he's cut it, but he's now sporting a Beatle-style mop top. "You and me!" he shouts, interrupting his manic shadowboxing, his hair flopping around on his forehead. "Yes? You and me!"

I smile as politely as possible, but I have no idea what he means. If it's an invitation to spar, he's asking the wrong person: it's the trainer who decides who spars with who. If he means you and me, maybe we go out for drinks later, it's also an invitation best not dignified with an answer.

Arturo is just now getting out of the ring as I cross over

to find my favorite jump rope from the cabinet, the one adorned with red-and-white-plastic beads. Arturo is so wet with sweat, he looks as if he's just come from a swimming pool; Gigo escorts him to the heavy bags, carrying a water bottle. As Arturo passes me, he smiles and extends his glove for me to touch with my own fist in greeting. This makes me absurdly happy: it's exactly what all of the guys do here amongst themselves. The lingering grin on my face embarrasses me. It seems preposterous to feel so elated— and so moved—by this small gesture of recognition.

Gilbert watches me skip rope and applauds politely when I cross my arms and slash the rope in front of me, a mild bit of hotdogging. Surprised at this acknowledgment, as unreserved praise is so rare here, I smile with pride. Skipping rope was the only activity in boxing familiar to me, and my childhood expertise came back quickly: experience with a jump rope was the one advantage in being a girl. I already knew a weighted cord is easier to maneuver than a plain rope. It requires far less energy to make a complete revolution. The heft of the long hollow beads surrounding the thin cord keeps the jump rope away from you in a more perfect orbit, which means there's less chance of getting a foot caught and tripping. Hours of skipping rope with my best friend on our back patio in Virginia taught me well.

Replacing the rope in the cabinet, I hand Gilbert my wraps. He's nervous binding my hands, fumbling. "This too tight?" he asks. The material gapes between my fingers. If I dropped my arm, it would spiral off my hand into a puddle of fabric. I glance around for Gigo, who's busy across the room, wiping Arturo's face with a towel. It looks like I'm Gilbert's responsibility today.

"Make it tighter," I tell him. "You'd better start over, and really wrap my wrists, too." My wrists are overly flexible, which makes them the weak link in my arm. Hector's method of wrapping my hands takes this problem into account, and by the time he locks down the Velcro fasteners at the end of the wrap around each wrist, my forearms and fists are fused into a single unit; strong, tight, secure.

Gilbert tries again, and with my guidance, we eventually arrive at a close approximation of Hector's expert handiwork. While shadowboxing, I glance around and wonder whom I'll spar with. By some odd coincidence, all of my usual sparring partners are finished in the ring and have moved on to the speed bag or the heavy bag. Arturo is alternating rounds on the heavy bag. In between rounds, Gigo throws a medicine ball hard into his abdomen, simulating body blows.

Crossing back to Gilbert, it occurs to me he isn't skilled enough to work with me on the mitts. I see Dominick prancing around in the ring, slashing his wrapped fists at phantoms. He seems to be my one option for a workout.

"Gilbert," I say quietly, my back to Dominick, "keep an eye on us, okay? I've sparred with him before, and I think he really likes to hurt people."

"Hey," Gilbert says, addressing Dominick, "you spar with her, but go easy on the lady, okay?"

Dominick lights up at the prospect of a fight. He eagerly hops down from the ring and digs his gloves and his duct-taped headgear out of a filthy blue gym bag. Squatting, he continues to rummage around in it for a while. "My mouth-guard," he says almost cheerfully. "It's okay, I can fight without it."

"Now you know where to hit him," says Gilbert softly, tightening the laces on my gloves.

Ducking under the ropes, I stare down for a moment at the bloodstained canvas. Gilbert reaches over the ropes and slides on my headgear. Unsure of which hole in the chinstrap is the correct one, he overtightens it at first, catching a thin fold of flesh from my neck in the buckle. "Not so tight. One back," I gasp. Dominick has wrapped his own hands himself and uses gloves with elastic at the wrists that are easy to pull on without any help. He stands before me, smiling as if he's staring at dinner on the table. His irises have no color: the dark pools make a shocking contrast to his pale, slightly freckled skin. Glancing over at Gilbert, I smile nervously. The bell rings.

We touch gloves, and I immediately prepare myself for his favorite punch, the wild swinging left hook. It arrives on schedule, and my quick upraised block is successful. After that, he's all over the place, arms flailing out, tucking back; it's only because he favors long, swinging approaches that I have a prayer of blocking punches or getting out of his way. I land a couple of body shots, and we get in close to one another. In the ensuing scuffle, I feel his shoe beneath mine: I'm standing on it. This "mirror image problem" is an occupational hazard when it comes to fighting lefties: he's leading with his right foot, which is in constant opposition to my left leading foot, and sooner or later, toes are going to overlap. The lump beneath my sneaker feels wrong. It's not like stepping on another shoe, or a rock; it's alive. His foot thrashes beneath mine as he tries to tug it away, but the way his fists pull back for a moment shows how precariously off-balance he is, and I'm suddenly worried that he'll fall. I don't immediately smash him in the center of the chest for fear of the retaliation I would be due for knocking him down. A guy sensitive to issues of "respect" from a sparring partner wouldn't look upon that sort of opportunism, or "dirty" boxing, as fair game. I pull my foot away and hop backward quickly; if he still falls, maybe I'll be far enough away not to be considered responsible.

He recovers his balance and boils over in agitated energy, crouching down and bolting toward me at a run. I'm ready with a hard right to his mouth, and for a brief moment, I wonder if his teeth will tear the leather of my glove. One of his swinging left hooks checks me in the ear, a mildly stunning sensation, as I contemplate the health of my glove. I make him chase me around until I can recover, which in this case is until the bell rings.

My temples throb with each heartbeat. Gilbert removes my mouthpiece, and I have a crazy thought that there's not enough air in the room. Gilbert looks into my eyes with a concern I've never seen from Hector. "How are you doing? Want to stop?"

This question is so unthinkable, so shocking that I can only repeat the word. "Stop?"

"You okay?"

"Yes," I gasp, pointing to the water bottle. Jesus, he's going to embarrass me with his solicitous behavior. I look over at Dominick, who dances around alone, hopping back and forth. He's not even taking any water. He smiles at me and smashes his gloves together. I turn away and look at the direction of the windows: sky, soothing sky. Lots of air, lots of space.

The bell rings again, too soon. Biting down on my mouthpiece, it occurs to me I should be hitting him in the face more, as he's vulnerable without that piece of plastic. He storms over to me and lets fly a quick flurry of punches with that same manic energy I've seen in his shadow-boxing. Each punch is sharp, like a long, thin knife sliding in. Some boxers throw punches that feel blunt, like the dull end of a sledgehammer; the pain is distributed and yet still mighty. Dominick's punches are all razors and homemade shivs. I catch him in the face twice—he shakes his head and smiles each time. Whether his smile is really a grimace, I'm not sure, but whatever it is, it's scary to see.

We dance around each other, lunging forward and back

with quick jabs, and now it's my turn to have my foot stepped on. I try to jerk it away, but the little bastard actually leans all of his weight onto it and pounds away at me. I'm now trapped, cornered, completely captive. My forearms shield my upper chest and face, and as I struggle to pull away, I feel in danger of falling backward like a tree. My balance is so off that I'm afraid to even turn or twist as a defensive move. *Where is Gilbert?*

A sharp left uppercut just misses my jaw, and I clutch it hard to my chest, holding on with both hands. My face is suddenly vulnerable to his free right hand, so I lean my head into him, putting my chin well over his left shoulder; we're closer than we would be if I gave him a hug. His foot is still firmly planted on mine as his arm thrashes against my breasts like a fish. I inhale the tang of old sweat rising out of his T-shirt, the mildewed aroma of his headgear. I want to scream in panic for Gilbert, for the police, for my mother. I manage to yell "Get off my foot! My *foot*! Get off my foot, you *fucking* asshole!"

"Sorry!" he says, not sorry at all, and shifts his weight back, releasing me, pulling back his arm. Lurching backward, nearly falling from the sudden freedom, I skip away to catch up with the momentum. A few spectators have gathered, presumably alerted to the dirty dealings by my yelling. Gilbert is anxiously peering in through the ropes: was he just standing there mute the whole time? Next to him is a burly trainer I've seen here before, a soft-spoken black man who is watching me with a worried expression;

deep furrows are carved into his forehead, and his lips are puckered in apprehension. I race toward Dominick, furious: I should have let the little asshole fall when I was standing on his foot. I should have smashed him in the chest when I had the chance. Respect! Respect my goddamned, stepped-on foot! Our jabs crash together at the same time, as if I've thrown a punch into a mirror. There's a reverberating, tuning-fork sensation at my elbow joint, as it hyperextends. He's thudding maniacally against my ribs, and I don't care. I'm busy flailing at his head, pounding at his face until the bell rings.

Stumbling heavily over to my corner, I hear the trainer chastising Gilbert: "They shouldn't be sparring! He hits too hard!" I'm breathing heavily, nearly groaning with each exhale, but too angry to be frightened.

"That fucking asshole! He was standing on my foot! Did you see that?"

"No! He was on your foot?" Gilbert says, wide-eyed. Either he's blind or a liar, but he's obviously saving face for not coming to my rescue and acting as referee.

"Fucking guy!" I lean on the ropes for a moment, something Hector would never have permitted. In Gleason's you rest between rounds on your feet. Having the little stool put out in your corner between rounds is a luxury reserved for an actual bout. The trainer has walked over to Dominick and is speaking to him in a low voice; Dominick is grinning at him crazily, like a bigmouthed, evil puppet.

I take long drinks of water as Gilbert tips the bottle into

my mouth. "You're doing great. Stay away from him as much as you can. Practice your defense." I look over and see that Arturo and Gigo have walked over to Dominick's side of the ring as well. The next round should be interesting.

The bell rings, and I hop over to him, arms down, to touch gloves. His fists are already raised, and he takes this golden opportunity to dish out a quick uppercut, a classic sucker punch. My chin rockets up and to the left, and a burning sensation in the back of my shoulder pours up into my neck like hot liquid. I hop backward, staring incredulously at him, before inhaling sharply to fire off a five-punch combination: jab, right, right uppercut, left hook, and then the only one that really lands with any power, a hard right to his ribs. Twisting off my right toe as I land it, I can feel the skin tear away on the bottom of my foot: another blister frayed to hell. I can hear someone yelling "Don't hit so hard!"

Are they talking to me? I risk a glance ringside. It's the trainer, staring angrily at Dominick. I dance backward, to give Dominick a chance to see that he's the one being yelled at. "Don't—hit—so—hard!"

Dominick looks over briefly and says nothing. We tangle again into a clinch. I can feel him shifting his foot around, trying to stand on mine. "Don't do it," I snarl, struggling to free one of my hands from his bear hug around my torso. "Get off me!"

We break apart, and he lands yet another left hook into my cheekbone, then follows it with a hard shot to my stomach, knocking most of the wind out of me: "Ooof." Shots to the stomach are always a miserable surprise.

"Don't hit so hard!" The trainer is bellowing again. *"Don't hit so hard!"* As I struggle to inhale, I'm wondering if this trainer will climb into the ring with us. I would love to chime in that he is indeed hitting me too hard, but that's out of the question. If other people say you're being hit too hard, it proves you're tough, but if you're the one pointing it out, you lack heart. As horrible as I feel at this moment, it would be—*unseemly* to complain about it.

The trainer resumes his mantra. "Don't—hit—so—hard!" The round warning bell has sounded, indicating that there's only thirty seconds before the end of the rounds, and this flat buzzer seems to electrify Dominick.

I never saw the punch coming, but if a target were painted on my face, it landed in the bull's-eye, squarely, flatly into my nose. If his other punches felt like knives, this one felt as wide and broad as a two-by-four. All I can remember is his over-the-top grin right before it happened.

"Oh! Oh, oh, oh, oh, oh." This is the sound I hear after the punch lands, and I notice, somehow, as if from a great distance, that the voice sounds exactly like my own. Somehow I've moved quickly away, my feet on autopilot, as if backpedaling on a unicycle. There's a warm, numbing, yet tingling sensation in my nose and upper lip; it's spreading out through my sinuses, radiating through the center of my face. Wet liquid is dripping, now pouring, onto my face. Snot? Or blood? I have a mild cold, so it's possible this is nothing more than a runny nose; that punch might have dislodged something in my sinuses.

Dominick is standing at the far side of the ring. It's as if I'm looking at him through the wrong end of a pair of binoculars. He's just hanging there, standing perfectly still, suspended. There's no noise, nothing.

Something turns over in my mind, a childish thought: He *ruined* everything. We were having such a good time, and then he had to *ruin* it. The guy couldn't let it alone, he went *too far*, and then he *ruined* everything. Warm liquid is pouring down my chin. Blood. It must be blood. Rage propels me across the ring, fists swinging. Dominick looks stunned to see me, then settles for blocking my punches. If it is blood on my face, I don't want anyone to say I just stood there cowering, too freaked out to fight. The spectators are making some sort of uproar. The bell rings.

I slowly stagger toward my corner to see that Gilbert is climbing into the ring. I raise a glove to my throbbing nose and feel the leather slide against my face, which is weirdly slick. I pull it away and stare at my glove, shocked.

Even against the dull black, it looks too bright and too red; it looks so terribly wrong, my blood. My eyes look down the front of my white T-shirt, which is splattered in blood. And blood is still falling out of my face in heavy, pregnant drops like summer rain. One splashes against the canvas, another on my bare thigh, leaving a red trail as it rolls toward my knee; now I'm moving forward, craning my neck forward, trying to bleed on the canvas, rather than on myself. Gilbert has arrived and is pulling my headgear off. As he does this, I have nothing to do but stare at these big droplets falling down and hitting the floor, and I'm starting to lose it. There's a big clog of crying working against my chest wall, fighting to bust out in a series of panicked, wracking sobs. I'm upset and scared, but I'm more afraid of everyone else knowing how scared I am. I had my ribs smashed a while ago, and here I am, afraid of the sight of my own blood!

Gilbert reaches over to my mouth to remove my mouth-piece. The bright red color against the neon yellow plastic looks absurdly garish, the colors clash and vibrate, and I have to look away; it's making me queasy. There's a horrible taste in my mouth, the hot copper flavor of blood, as unnerving as chewing on aluminum foil. And while I've tasted blood before, this time I'm swallowing it, drinking it.

"No hard feelings," I say to Gilbert as we get down out of the ring.

"He hurt your feelings?"

"No!" I'm aware that everyone in the whole place has clustered around us, "I said, *'No hard feelings!'*" Getting this sporting, casual, terribly calculated sentence out without sobbing was a herculean task. That it might be misquoted into the girly observation that someone had hurt my feelings was, under the circumstances, intolerable. I'd rather bleed to death right here on the spot.

I'm rushed over to a folding chair by several pairs of hands. Some people are offering towels, others bottles of water. While I remain focused on not crying, I'm stunned by the generosity. One boxer hands me a towel soaked with ice water and holds it firmly up against my nose. *He's not afraid of me* is the random thought that floats through my brain. I'm bleeding all over the place, and no one's putting on rubber gloves. No one has considered the possibility that I could be HIV positive, a consideration that, if the situation were reversed, might give me pause.

Gigo steps forward and starts unlacing my gloves. "What are you doing?" I ask him, suddenly embarrassed by everyone's concern. "It's just a nosebleed. I still have three rounds with the heavy bag."

"No, no," he says, yanking off the gloves. "You do the speed bag first. Better for you."

I glance around and am surprised by the expressions on everyone's faces: shock, concern, horror, dismay. There's something oddly funny about it. Next time I want everyone to know I'm hurt by a punch in the ring, I should bite down on a vial of fake blood, and presto! Instant sympathy! Oh, the tragedy reflected in these usually impassive faces, as they behold me with a bloody nose. Such outrage! Just sitting here with a stained shirt, holding a soggy towel, I'm breaking everyone's hearts. People are taking turns pulling

Dominick aside, talking to him sternly, shaking his shoulders when he shrugs them by way of responding. Arturo dodges in past Gigo and Gilbert and leans toward me, touching my arm. "Lynn! From now on, you spar with me, okay?" I smile a little and nod, amused that everyone thinks I'm about to quit, that I'll get up and stomp on out of here. At least three boxers have leaned in to tell me not to blow my nose, to just let it alone.

Dominick steps forward and stands in front of me. He's smiling. "Hey . . . !" His arms are outstretched, as if I'm invited to stand up and embrace him.

"Look, I'm fine. You got a lucky punch, that's all." My voice sounds like I have a bad cold. The blood's probably clotting.

"Nothing lucky about it," Gilbert says quietly, some anger in his tone, his hand protectively on my shoulder. "It was a punch."

"You . . . hit me," Dominick says, his voice halting. "I hit you—you hit me, you hit hard! You know? I hit—I don't . . ." His voice trails off again. He's obviously been prodded into apologizing, but what he's doing is trying to tell me the bloody nose was my own fault. Well, it was. I am, after all, a boxer, in Gleason's. I did drag in my completely nonthreatening boyfriend, who told all assembled, including Dominick, that I could take care of myself. I wanted to learn how to be a killer, and now there's a cluster of men here who want Dominick to apologize to me for taking undue advantage. I came in here to be treated equally, and to kick ass, and suddenly I feel a little too much like his poor victim sitting here covered in blood.

Standing slowly, I walk over to the equipment locker and get a speed bag. The assembled group looks awkwardly after me as I pass. Still holding the bloody towel under my nose, I cross the room and hook up the bag. The cluster of boxers at the now-empty folding chair has broken up. The show's over.

The bell rings, and I carefully lay the towel down on a relatively clean stretch of floor. The pressure in my sinuses when I bend over squeezes tears out of my eyes. A small sound of pain comes out of my mouth. Straightening up again, I inhale slowly through my mouth and get to work. Pounding the speed bag is a relief, an activity that doesn't require tremendous effort, speech, or the appearance of bravery. While no one's talking to me, I still feel everyone's eyes.

"Excuse me. Miss?" It's the trainer who was doing all the yelling at ringside. "You should go to the bathroom," he says gently. "Clean up your nose."

"Okay," I say, continuing to hit the bag. I'll go during a round break. If I go now, it'll look like I can't wait, that I feel faint or am rushing in there to puke. As I hit the bag, I can hear this trainer talking to another boxer, an enormous heavyweight with biceps the size of my thighs. He's working a speed bag next to me, and his shaved head has the color and shine of burnished ebony. He's stopped now and has dropped the headphones of the Walkman he's wearing around his tree-trunk neck to hear what his trainer is telling him. The earpieces are poking into his flesh, creating small dimples in the vast expanse of smooth skin. I can't quite hear what the trainer is saying, but I'm pretty sure he's talking about me and what just happened in the ring.

The buzzer sounds, and I walk to the locker room, dabbing at my face with the bloody towel to convey the message: *I guess I'll just pop in here for a second, freshen up a little.*

My face in the mirror looks unreal, as if I'm covered in cheap stage blood. I've never seen this much of my own blood before. A small amount is smeared around my face, but my nostrils are encrusted with it. I flare them experimentally; they're still mostly numb, but I can feel the skin shift as the dried blood crackles. To my relief, my nose still appears to be straight. Gingerly feeling my way down from the bridge to the tip, it seems, under the swelling, whole and sturdy, not broken. Tipping my head back, I see what the trainer must have been referring to, what anyone would want to know about: two large, dark blood clots hanging out of each nostril. "Oh, God, *disgusting*," I can't help but blurt out, as I carefully wipe one out into the sink with a damp paper towel. Lying there in the running water, it looks like some sort of amphibious creature, a slimy, blood-colored tree frog. Closing my eyes for a moment— my eyelids ache when I squeeze them together, he must have caught me there, somehow—I run the cold water hard and splash my face with it. I hear the bell ring for the next round as I gently pat myself dry. Smoothing my hair back, I fix a barrette to catch a stray damp lock of hair and notice a pale blue bruise near the outside corner of my right eye, no doubt from one of his left hooks. So much for the vaunted protection of headgear. I grab the bloody towel and hurry back out.

"Who did this?" says the heavyweight, jutting his chin at me. His absurdly large hand rests on my speed bag to prevent me from using it until I've told him what he wants to know. His trainer's eyewitness account wasn't enough apparently, and he waits for confirmation.

"Um, Dominick. That guy over there," I say, gesturing with my head and eyes rather than pointing. Dominick is flailing away at a heavy bag, shoulders hunched, head down.

"You shouldn't have to fight that guy," says the trainer. "It's not right what he does. I saw him do this to someone else, a young kid. He does that with anyone he thinks is weaker. He fights dirty, simple as that."

"Really," the boxer says. "I should lay the motherfucker out."

I shrug my shoulders with feigned indifference to this offer, but I really wanted to say, "Gee, would you please?" Turning back to my speed bag, there's a metallic squeak to my left: Gilbert has set up the folding chair for himself about five feet from where I'm standing. "You gave that guy a good bruise."

"Really? Where?"

"Here," he says, smiling, pointing to the area below his left eye, near his cheekbone.

"Good. Motherfucking bastard." I pound the ball, finding a pocket of anger and releasing it. Gilbert laughs and drums along with my pounding on the chair.

"You know what he's saying? He's saying you hit hard! That's why he hit you! Everyone's telling him he hit you too hard, he stood on your foot, and he's saying 'But she hit me too hard! Talk to her about it!' "

"No!" I stop hitting the bag for a moment, stunned and pleased. A smile tugs at my aching face.

"I'll tell you what's going to happen," says Gilbert. "He's getting his ass kicked. I already heard a few guys saying they were going to teach him a boxing lesson." Gilbert laughs, and I join in. As a dirty fighter in here, Dominick now has the status of child molester in the prison: the lowest of the low.

When my gloves are laced back on, I'm grateful that Gilbert has cleaned the blood off the leather. I hand him the bloody towel, and he leads me over to work the heavy bag for three rounds. My entire head feels as if it's swelling, from the back of my head to the tip of my nose.

After carefully finishing the rest of my workout, I retreat to the locker room. Sitting on the floor, I drag my purse out from the bottom of my locker into my lap. When I find the small bottle of Advil, I shake two round brown tablets into my palm. Studying them a moment, I tip out another and

161

pop them into my mouth, dry. Then I hoist myself up and head for the sink. Gulping a mouthful of water from the tap, I stare again at my reflection. The pale blue bruise near my eye has bloomed into purple, the varicolored skin is swollen and stretched tight. The underside of my nose is a triangle of dark red with purple streaks leading to my upper lip. When I flick dried blood away from the inside of one nostril, my eyes tear—my fingernail has scraped against the delicate tissue. The numbness has disappeared, and now there's only pain.

An hour from now, I'll be meeting with a photography expert at Sotheby's with this face. There is an auction two days hence, and I'm hoping there might be a picture I can afford. The meeting was set up weeks ago. I can't cancel.

I had forgotten about this meeting when I hurriedly dressed this morning, so I'm wearing black jeans, a small blue T-shirt, and black leather sandals. My gym clothes, including the bloodstained T-shirt, are in a compartment of an oversized black satchel that drags down my right shoulder. Gently sliding on my sunglasses, I check the mirror to see if they camouflage my injuries. The bruised eye is mostly concealed, but my nose and slightly swollen upper lip stand out like a beacon. The glasses won't hide a thing, so I slip them into my purse and steel myself.

Walking through the doors of Sotheby's, I feel sloppy and out of place, not to mention sore, bruised, and bloodied. The receptionist is wearing a crisp linen shirt, her manicured nails, painted the palest of pinks, tapping delicately into the telephone keypad. So perfectly neat, so glamorous at four o'clock on a Friday afternoon.

While I awkwardly stand by and wait for Susan, the photography expert, a woman in her fifties breezes past, waving to the receptionist, carrying with her a cloud of Chanel No. 5, my mother's favorite. I listen to the heels of her black leather pumps *click click click* on the marble floor. Her hair, a mound of blond spun floss, is tucked back into a chignon; her dress is closed with an invisible zipper, and the pull tag dangles down in the center of her back like a tiny pendant. There goes the type of woman who wears nylons all summer, who goes to the hairdresser's every week, who never breaks a sweat unless she's out in the back garden tending to her roses. Suddenly I hear a voice behind me.

"Nice to meet you," says Susan, another attractive, put-together woman, in her twenties. Her eyes fly around my face, unsure of where to land. I try desperately to think of plausible explanations: *Oh! I see you're looking at my face! It's nothing really, I was in a minor car accident. It's silly, actually, I slipped in the shower. Oh, I fell down the stairs. That'll teach me to wear high heels while drinking. I was mugged three blocks from here, but it's okay, the police got him.* "I was sparring this afternoon," I say finally, resigned to the truth. "Hey, you should see the other guy!" I laugh, but she looks confused. "Boxing. It's nothing. I'm fine. It looks worse than it feels. Probably."

"You box?" she says a little too politely.

"How long have you worked here?" I ask as we walk inside. Later, as I stand in a gallery and examine a Joel-Peter Witkin photograph, it dawns on me that her gentle tone of voice means she thinks I was beaten up by a boyfriend or husband. She thinks I'm a battered woman.

PROTECTION

I HAD WANTED to learn how to fight like the men at Gleason's. Now I was starting to think like them. A man should be infuriated if another man messes with his woman. Dominick messed with me; where was Eli? I had become so co-opted by the primitive value systems in the gym, that suddenly it made sense for a man—my man—to intervene on my behalf.

The night after the fight I lie on the couch with an ice pack pressed to my face. My feet are in Eli's lap. "You've got to go back," I tell him, my voice muffled. "You have to at least *act* mad in front of them."

"What do you want me to do, fight this guy?"

"Look, it's real simple. You have to go in and act really, really—*offended*. Someone fucked around with your woman! You don't have to actually get into the ring. The important thing is that they *believe* that you would fight. That you're *demanding* to fight this guy who damaged your property! That's everything."

"So what should I do, go in there and say 'Hey, Dominick, you and me, step outside'?"

"No, then he might step outside! And you're fucked!"

"You don't think I could take this guy in a fight?"

"Look, here's what you do," I say, sitting up, setting the ice pack aside. "And by the way, no, you can't take him in a fight. I should know. You walk in and go like this when you see him." Standing, I swagger toward a phantom Dominick, who I imagine to be standing at my aquarium. My head leads in front of my body, but my chest is puffed out, and my hands dangle at my sides like a gunfighter, ready to draw. "Then you say"—I drop my voice lower, quietly, slowly addressing my fish—" 'You stay away from her. I ever hear you go near her again . . .' Then, and this is very important, *do not* finish the sentence. Just don't ever say what you'll do! You say you'll beat the crap out of him, he'll want to fight you on the spot! This way he doesn't know what you're threatening. You might have a friend in mind, someone who will shoot him on the street when he comes

out of the gym. Believe me, it'll be a lot more effective if
you just act like you're unbelievably steamed, but you do
not lay out your plans for punishment. Just glare at him.
Look angry, as if what you feel is beyond words." I walk
back over to the couch and pick up the ice pack, pressing
it to my face. "Okay? You think you can handle that? You
can do that for me?"

"You want me to do this," he says, not as a question.
"You think it's going to help you. You don't want anyone to
touch you, ever again, in there."

"It's not that. It's that for this sort of thing to happen"—
I gesture at the ice pack—"and my boyfriend doesn't react
to it? It's *weird.* To them, it's weird. I need you to react to it.
You need to look like you're mad at this guy." Frustrated
that he still doesn't get it, I feel tears threatening in the
back of my throat. "There are guys there who are more upset about what happened than you are! Guys I don't even
know! I don't even know their *names*, and they're planning
to kick his ass for what he did to me!" My voice quavers a
little, touched at what these boxers, these strangers, will do
to Dominick. "If you can't come in and at least *pretend* to
be outraged . . ." I let the sentence hang, and we both know
what I'm threatening, which is *don't bother ever coming
over here again.*

Monday morning, Eli accompanies me to the gym. We
barely speak on the subway; I'm more nervous than he is.
If he screws up this time, I have to get a new boyfriend to
show up at the gym, no two ways about it.

Eli and I have taken five steps inside of Gleason's when I see Dominick interrupting his workout to rush over. Loping toward us, he carries the manic energy of an unruly dog desperate for attention. Dominick is wearing his usual wolfish smile, but Eli plays his part well and only glowers back. "You stay away from her," he says, pointing a finger. For my part, I'm suddenly afraid I'll burst out in nervous, incredulous laughter over how absurdly important this charade is to me.

"What, you mad at me?" Dominick says, surprised. Evidently he was expecting us to greet him like a brother. "You want to fight me? You want to fight?" To my relief, Eli doesn't say no. And to my even greater relief, he doesn't say yes. Dominick quickly switches gears from surprise to incredulity and now resentment. "You mad at me? You should be mad at *her*!"

"Oh, shut up." To my surprise, this outburst comes from me.

"I hear about you fighting her again . . ." Eli says, glaring mightily. He makes fists out of both of his hands as they dangle by his side. I can see a few boxers snickering at this encounter, but they stop when they see my reaction to it: I look ashamed, tugging at Eli's arm, asking him to sit down, reassuring him that I'm fine, begging him to go. My distress gives his anger credibility.

Hector, roused by the minor commotion, leaves his spot near the equipment locker and walks over.

"Hector, welcome back," I tell him, morose. "Too bad

you weren't here last week," I say, pointing at my still-bruised nose.

Ignoring the standoff between the men, Hector takes my chin in his hand and whistles. He slowly turns my head from side to side, inspecting the damage, and smiles. She's hurt and she still came back! That he's not asking me any questions means he knows exactly what happened.

"Ho-kay," he says cheerfully. "Get dress."

As Hector turns away, I step over to Eli, preventing him from following. "Leave," I tell him. "Seriously," my voice low. "Just leave, go to that restaurant across the street and down the alley. I'll meet you there in an hour or so. Act like you're furious with me for wanting to spar right now."

"You want to spar?" he says, raising his voice.

"Not too loud. It's better if they can't hear what you're saying. Just be angry."

"You want to get the crap beaten out of you again?" His teeth are gritted, his jaw tight. "Well, I won't be responsible! Anyone touches you . . ." and with that, he stomps out.

Still facing the door, I exhale slowly, willing the tension to leave along with him. If he had stayed, it would have been unlikely he could have kept up that performance. There was bound to be a moment when he laughed, smiled at me, or cracked a joke. Turning around, I pick up my gym bag and walk toward the locker room.

Hector is standing with a man who looks to be about thirty years old, with pale freckled skin and reddish sandy hair. His broad, muscular build makes him look stocky, his decision to weight-train only emphasizing what he wishes would be overlooked: the fact that he's only about five foot six. He's wearing baggy, drawstring army green pants, the preferred fashion option for a man whose thighs are now too large in proportion to his hips to wear pants off the rack. A pale gray T-shirt strains against his bulging chest. He's carefully cuffed up the short sleeves and stands with his arms crossed, flaunting his biceps.

"Thees guy, he fight in the Garden!" says Hector.

"Hi, I'm Terry," he says, offering me his huge hand.

"Hi, I'm Lynn."

"She hits," says Hector with a laugh, "like an *animal!*" He fans his face with his hand, as if he's been the recipient of one of my blows.

"Yeah?" says Terry, rearing back on his heels a little, flexing his neck.

"I do my best," I tell him, looking down at him. Every encounter tests dominance.

"Ho-kay!" Hector claps his hands together. "Today you fight thees guy, where is he. Heem. Eric." He nods over at a tall, lanky black teenager skipping rope in the corner. Built more for a basketball court than a boxing ring, he moves with the gawkiness that accompanies a growth spurt. As he struggles with the rope, shoulders hunched, eyes downcast, he carries the guilty resignation of one who's been put here as a punishment.

Emerging from the locker room a few minutes later, I pass a few boxers who were here on Friday. They nod in silent greeting; I nod back. Coming back on Monday scores more points than not crying on Friday.

Gilbert sees me and waves, gesturing at his face, then pointing at mine, a silent inquiry about my injuries. I nod and shrug my shoulders as he walks over.

"Hey," he says. "Your friend got . . ."

"What?"

"Arturo and Dominick sparred on Saturday. Dominick didn't do so well," he says, laughing, slapping me on the arm. His voice is low. "It was bad, it was bad."

"He looks okay to me."

"I hear Arturo knocked him down. It lasted like, one round. I wasn't here, I just heard about it." Hector glares at me from across the room: too much chatter, not enough action. I pick up my pace and head for the equipment locker to grab a jump rope. Boxers nod at me as I pass.

Stepping up into the ring, Hector straps on my headgear. *Why bother* is the thought that floats by; it sure didn't protect me from injury last week. My swollen temple throbs momentarily against a shift of the leather. After sliding in my mouthguard, Hector walks over to Eric's corner and does the same. The slow dawn of realization that this order is usually reversed now breaks: Is it the novice who gets served last? Have I graduated?

The bell rings. Eric and I come out of our corners and meet in the center, gloves outstretched. He towers over me as he gently, tentatively, touches my gloves, and I experience a slight rubbing sensation through my wraps. Hopping back once as an official start, I leap forward with an upper-cut. He fumbles it away, giggling soundlessly, his face open in silent mirth, his shoulders shaking in laughter. The ignominy of being paired with a girl? As he laughs, I sock him square in the face with a hard right.

"Why you laughing!" Hector bellows from the sidelines. Eric darts away, skittering to my left, his arms wide; I half-expect him to be dribbling a ball. Turning to follow, I throw jab after jab. Most connect, and his response is to leap backward. The pressure of repeatedly leaping after him and stopping short has set the balls of my feet on fire from friction. The big toe on my left foot is hot on its right edge and is swelling with every shift. The Band-Aid has peeled off on the underside and has rolled into a small cigarette between my toes. With luck, the gauze should still protect the place where my nail was.

Landing a hard right into Eric's ribs, he smiles and shakes his head. His grin is of embarrassment, and it occurs to me, as the warning buzzer sounds, that he has yet to lay a hand on me.

"You can hit me," I tell him, annoyed. We dodge around each other, and he finally throws a tentative jab, which I knock down.

"Fight!" Hector yells. Eric looks in Hector's direction and drops his hands. Correcting my stance, I throw a right into his jaw as hard as I can.

"Ooooowwwww!" Hector crows in admiration. *Look where you fighting, Eric.* Taking two hard steps backward, Eric threatens to topple. I lean in and hammer at his ribs. He grabs me in an embrace, his arms draping over my shoulders like a lead stole. My upper arms are pinned, my gloves flail uselessly.

"Get off me!" I gasp. He grabs me tighter, pressing down, regaining his balance as if I'm a buoy and he's a drowning man. "Get off me!" I shout louder, and then the bell rings. He releases me with another goofy grin.

"Get out of the ring," Hector says to Eric. "What you do yesterday? You should be running! Look at you, tired already!" Hector turns to a fat, hulking, thirty-five-year-old marshmallow slowly shadowboxing at the sidelines. "You! Two rounds!"

Swallowing water, I watch my new opponent slowly duck under the ropes. He's already breathing hard, but each of his arms looks like a leg of beef. If he lays those on my shoulders and leans forward, my knees are going to buckle. Eric shrugs his shoulders as he hops down from the ring. Casual indifference or the release of tension? Gilbert unlaces his gloves and hands him a speed bag.

My opponent nods at me, and I remember that he's someone I've only seen working the heavy bag, a big brute who stands still and slugs. "Jab, jab," says Hector, putting in my mouthpiece. "Move aroun'." I get the message: Run him to death.

It might have been easier if we had been out in the open, just running, as I would have outdistanced him in a hurry. But this wise grizzly bear uses the ring like a chessboard, anticipating moves, blocking them, and then check-mate: cornered, with a 250-pound man on top of me. After just such a claustrophobic encounter, where I had the sudden urge to kick him in the shin after flailing at him with an uppercut, I learned not to get too close. It occurs to me that in Hector-speak, "Jab, jab" might mean "stay as far away from him as the distance of your outstretched arm, and use the jab to prevent him from getting any closer." A flicker of annoyance crosses my face as I consider his policy of brevity. Why the big mystery?

The big bear throws a jab that flattens my nose; the tear-inducing, eye-clenching pain causes me to yelp. "Sorry!" he says, aghast.

"My fault," I say, feeling ridiculous for causing my opponent to apologize for doing exactly what he's supposed to do.

When the round ends and we get out of the ring, the bear says, "You have a good right. I really felt it."

"Thank you," I say. Hector removes my headgear, and I jump down. "Did Arturo fight Dominick this past Saturday?" I ask Hector as he removes my gloves.

"What?" he says, pausing for a moment, confused. "Arturo no' here."

"I know, I mean, on Saturday. Did he come in and train on Saturday?"

"No," he says, his eyes narrowing with suspicion. "Why you asking?"

"Gilbert told me he heard he was here, and that he sparred

with Dominick, and that he knocked Dominick down." My enthusiasm for providing details is rapidly draining with each moment that Hector stares at me. "Something like that." Hector is silent as he hands me the speed bag: the discussion is over.

Later Hector sits on a bench next to the equipment locker and watches me skip rope. He chuckles briefly before bursting forth in a high, quavery singing voice, "Arturo's in love with you." He laughs again. "He's in looooove weeeeeeth youuuuuu." Deciding not to bite, I hang up my jump rope and head for the locker room.

When I emerge, Hector is still at his spot on the bench, supervising Eric on the jump rope. As I hand Hector his pay for this week, he grabs my wrist and laughs again. "Arturo's in love with you." There's a threat beneath the chuckle, as if he's caught me cheating on him.

LEGACY

BOXERS ARE TRAINED, indeed encouraged, to be aggressive and violent. The best athletes react instantly, and winning can depend upon a split-second decision. The will to be violent is an unfortunate combination of nature and nurture. First you have the way, then you have the means. And if you're paid to be violent and rewarded for it, and you're very good at it, it shouldn't be surprising that the real struggle would be in turning that instinct off when you get home.

Often, that struggle is lost. In 1924, boxer Charles "Kid"

McCoy was convicted of manslaughter in the death of his wife and spent seven years in San Quentin. Carlos Monzon, the world middleweight champion from 1970 until 1977, was sent to jail in 1989 after his girlfriend, Alicia Muniz, plummeted to her death from the balcony of his home. That same year, Josh Pompey—a former sparring partner for heavyweight champion Larry Holmes—murdered his ex-girlfriend and her seventy-four-year-old aunt. After breaking into their home, Pompey started choking the younger woman and pounding her face. When the aunt heard the commotion and came to the aid of her niece, Pompey punched her as well. He then stabbed both women several times.

More recently, former boxer Timothy Howard Harris was convicted of first-degree murder for gunning down the attorney who had represented Harris's ex-wife during their bitter divorce. Mike Tyson was convicted of raping a teenaged beauty pageant contestant in an Indianapolis hotel room in 1991, and served three years in prison. Upon his release, he lost his boxing license for one year after biting Evander Holyfield's ear in June of 1997, during their rematch. In February of 1999, Tyson pleaded no-contest to charges that he assaulted two motorists during a fender-bender. He was sentenced to one year in jail, but was paroled after serving less than four months. Once one of boxing's most promising young fighters, Tony Ayala Jr., was released from jail in 1999 after serving sixteen years, also for rape. And in that year, professional boxer Dezi Ford was convicted of involuntary manslaughter after beating his fourteen-month-old son to death. Admitting to the accident, Ford claimed that he had shadowboxed with the boy, but he had been playing. When the baby's mother came home, she found her son's eyes were rolled back and his tongue thrashing.

As I was learning, a boxer's training is extremely difficult to confine to the ring. Rational thought becomes secondary to impulse. The boxer *acts*.

I don't have to go to Gleason's today. On Thursdays I run five miles. There's no opponent and no Hector. Just me and Central Park. I used to hate the fall; it brought the start of school, the end of swimming pool season, and scratchy wool clothes; the depressing prospect of cold, messy weather. Since I've become a runner, however, I've revised my opinion of the cooler months. Early-autumn days are ideal for a jog through Central Park, that golden time when it's still possible to wear shorts, and the cooler conditions magically bestow greater athletic prowess; where it used to take me 42 labored minutes to run four miles, now it's an easy 39.

School is back in session, but at three-thirty in the afternoon, it's out for the day. Kids who've only been able to glimpse the perfect weather through classroom windows are now streaming into the park, carrying backpacks, sodas, laughing and pushing one another, and occasionally, the pungent smell of marijuana is carried on a breeze.

Cresting a hill on the west side, just past the reservoir, I see a group of high school boys on my side of the road, waiting to cross. There's a break in the traffic, but they hesitate when they see me running toward them. One of them murmurs something that makes the others quiet down.

My danger radar is screaming at me to veer off to the middle of the street and away from them, but as a runner, I hate breaking stride. Even dodging a pothole disturbs my pace, and after a mile or two, when I find that groove, where my legs are moving on the same, well-oiled track, it makes the miles effortlessly tick past like minutes on a clock. To be forced to change that rhythm might mean another half a mile of trying to find it again and maybe never succeeding. I've yelled at pedestrians to rein in their trip-wire dog leashes, at bikers who've stopped to chat and are blocking the lane entirely. I'll risk the embarrassment of these shrill outbursts just to prevent that critical loss of momentum. And so when I pass these boys, I'm tense, coiled, holding my breath: *Please* don't make me get out of my zone.

"Boooo!" One kid has leaped forward into my path, both hands up near his face, a mock bogeyman pose, as if he's about to reach out and grab me. He's probably all of fourteen, in baggy jeans and an enormous sweatshirt, with a bright open face and straight white teeth. At my height, he's not much of a threat, but that's not how I react in the split second when our paths cross.

My right hand shoots out and stiff-arms him backward,

my palm landing to the left of his sternum with a hard, hollow thump. He is on his way down as I pass, and judging from the noise and commotion, I can visualize his landing: surprised, undignified, humiliated, right on his rump, knees akimbo, backpack on the ground.

A collective howl rises up immediately, a war cry from his friends. My legs work a little harder, the adrenaline surge generated by fear. A male voice tears through the din:

"Take her *down*! Take her *down*!" Footsteps accelerate behind me. Horrified, I surge forward into a sprint. But my mind is strangely calm: *Not too fast.* An inner voice is rationalizing and planning. *You may have to run for a long time to get away. Don't look behind you, it's a waste of energy, and you'll slow down; just stay ahead of the footsteps, and you might outlast them.* I'm scanning the horizon for cars: Would one stop if I suddenly bolted into the road, arms raised? And then I think: *Why did you do that?* I could have easily avoided this situation. But I had to hit him.

The footsteps are loud behind me, but still not close; the kid is slamming his feet hard against the pavement, which means he doesn't run often. *Okay, I have a chance.* There's a fork in the road ahead; one leads into the park, the other to the exit. Will there be enough pedestrians on the sidewalk if I need help? And *will* they help? I can hear traffic coming toward me. The red light has finally changed. The park road it is. The tenets of feminism forgotten, I think:

Men drive cars. Men can help me with these kids. Maybe I can even hail a cab.

A moment or two passes before I risk a backward glance: the kid I pushed is now standing in the road, his hands on his knees, head up, catching his breath. He sees me looking and gestures at me with both hands in a giant dismissive wave. His friends are farther back, laughing and pointing. I slow up a little, but not for another quarter of a mile, when I'm sure that they can't see me, do I allow myself to finally slow down.

What, I wonder, have I become?

FEAR

THE PANIC ATTACKS begin three weeks later, just before a sparring episode with Eric, the tall, gawky teenager.
He's standing with his gloves down, waiting for the bell,
loosely rolling his head to and fro. So far, Eric's limited
his aggression to flurries of light jabs, content to practice
his defense with me, bobbing and weaving around my
punches.

I've never heard Eric speak. Boxers are not encouraged
to talk, whether it's to other boxers or to their trainers, but
over time I've begun to wonder if Eric is actually a mute.

Any questions I have for him as we step out of the ring together are answered with a single shrug, a slight good-
natured grimace, the universal "I don't know." Whether
the question is "Did I hurt you today?" or "How long have
you been boxing?" the answer is the same, which makes it
something of a private game to find a question that Eric
will have to answer verbally. Earlier, when Eric was skipping rope across the room, I asked Hector if he'd ever
heard him speak.

"No." Then the fact of Eric's silence dawned on him too.
This was the first time Hector and I communicated, the
first time we understood what the other was saying without
elaboration. I smiled with the pleasure of it.

"How do we know his name's Eric?" I said. "Did he tell
you?"

"Hees father. He came in with hees father." Hector
looked over at Eric and laughed a little. A mute, whether
by choice or necessity, is a trainer's dream.

Suddenly, standing in the ring with this sweet, mute boy,
I'm overwhelmed by a feeling of doom. I want to curl up on
the canvas and retch with anxiety. The sound of my heartbeat is echoing in my ears, and my mouthpiece is awash in
a flood of sour, bitter saliva. There's not enough oxygen in
the room. I'm breathing in short, ragged gasps. My skin is
clammy. The room tilts momentarily, then rights itself. A
wave of nausea roils through my guts. Focusing on the dirty
windows just beyond the ring, I blink hard, afraid of passing out. At the same time, I'm seized with a desperate urge

to run toward these sunlit panes of glass, or to take a hard right at the wall and bolt down the stairs. If I could just get outside, I could breathe again.

Somehow I try to quell this riot in my head. *What's the problem? There's plenty of air. It's just little old Eric over there, nothing to be afraid of.*

The bell rings, and Eric quickly turns his head in my direction. We lope toward each other and touch gloves. To my surprise, the urge to run has suddenly disappeared—the flames of panic have been doused by the reassurance in those familiar liquid eyes and the routine of sparring. We dance around for a bit, and an opening appears: his right arm has dropped, exposing his head. I rocket a left jab directly into his cheekbone.

He staggers back a step and smiles broadly, his white mouthpiece making little sucking noises against the intake of air; another giggle fit. "Put up you hands!" Hector yells. I jab again, and Eric blocks. We lumber through three rounds, and I never again connect as solidly, although he clocks me a few times in my left temple with his fast right hook. When I leave the gym that day, I dismiss my panic before sparring as an anomaly. Maybe it was something I ate. A full moon. The unconscious aftereffects of a bad dream.

It's not an anomaly. This horrible panic now grips me every time I step into the ring, even if I'm there alone to shadowbox. At home, lying in bed, I close my eyes and picture the view from the ring: the glare from the unwashed windows, the dust motes rising, the pale blue of the canvas. My chest tightens; my even breathing becomes shallow gasps. I pant under the covers until I talk myself down, convince myself that I'm really at home, alone, in bed, the door locked and bolted, the safest place in the world.

Over lunch I tell my friend Rosemary about this latest development. "Maybe you should quit already," she says. "This is getting crazy."

I consider the option of quitting for a brief second, to see if there's some point to be made about it. Boxers have quit before. One of the greatest, Sugar Ray Leonard, was forced to retire because of a detached retina. But the idea of walking away because I'm having *panic attacks* in the ring, before anyone lays a glove on me—no, it's too embarrassing to even contemplate. I shrug off the suggestion. "Oh, it's not that big a deal," I say. "Not worth quitting over, anyway." We pick at our salads and sip at small bottles of sparkling water. I stare at my bruised knuckles, purplish red in the sunlight, a pretty contrast to the thin, bright yellow flower that stands between us, soldier straight in its tiny vase.

———

My sister-in-law, Kathy, is a family therapist and suggests I try EMDR. It sounds like a drug, but it's more akin to hypnosis: eye movement desensitization and reprogramming. The theory is that a traumatic experience releases a hormone into the brain, norepinephrine, which causes the event to freeze in a constantly rerunning film. This results in post-traumatic stress syndrome, the cycle of being terrified by something that happened weeks, months, or years ago as if it just occurred. EMDR is based on the premise that this hormone causes the left and right hemispheres to become "misaligned," and if a trained therapist initiates rapid lateral eye movement in a patient, it resynchronizes the hemispheres, and the traumatic event can finally be processed in a normal way.

Three weeks after first panicking in the ring, I give EMDR a try and, indeed, the attacks do go away, but fear remains, as chilling as the chalk outline of a body after it has been removed. I no longer quake waiting for the bell to ring, but my breathing has a ragged, gasping undertone while I spar, a desperate sound. Sweating profusely during a workout is nothing new to me, but now there's a new twist: my sweat-soaked clothes smell of ammonia; the by-product of adrenaline, the scent of fear.

Some weeks later I notice Bruce with an older, white-haired gentleman in a dark blue suit who is affixing a business card to a bulletin board. He smiles as I walk past. Bruce introduces him as one Dr. Halpin.

Dr. Halpin is a hypnotist who works with Mike Tyson and other boxers, offering them an opportunity to "eliminate fear." Dr. Halpin's voice is firm yet soothing when he tells me this. "Many, many boxers suffer from fear in the ring," he says, waving a hand to indicate numbers too vast to be reckoned.

"Really! I thought it was just me." And I'm thrilled to find out it isn't.

"No one wants to admit it," he says, holding up a professional finger. "It's very widespread."

"So is Mike *Tyson* afraid when he's in the ring?"

"I've worked with Mike for many, many years. I fly out to have a session with him right before every fight." I take one of his cards, which says "Habit and Sports Hypnosis," and carefully put it in my wallet. "I also help people stop smoking and lose weight."

Later that same day, Hector puts me in the ring to spar with a new boxer in his stable. " 'e don't understand me," says his new charge, as we climb into the ring. "Do you understand me?"

Hector has nicknamed this boxer "the Empire State Building," but Rudy is from England, a black heavyweight with a Cockney accent that is entirely unintelligible to Hector. A professional with several fights to his name, Rudy was training elsewhere but has faith that Hector can turn him into the champion he believes he can be. But while Hector can train someone who never speaks, Rudy wants a trainer who will listen. So far Rudy's dry wit and running commentary have not endeared him to Hector, who is presently watching us talk with some suspicion.

The bell rings; we touch gloves. I can see why Hector picked the Empire State Building as a moniker, even if it is on the wrong continent: Rudy is tall, massive, immovable, and imposing. He's also a southpaw. Hector has briefed me on strategies with a left-handed fighter, how to come at them from their right, but now, hopping around him in the ring, I can't remember which side is which. I have a hard time telling left from right on a good day, when a punch to the face isn't a by-product of such misjudgment.

Rudy advances toward me and throws a right that I never see coming—there's just a brief sensation of my gloves being parted away from my head a microsecond before what feels like a skillet colliding with the side of my face. *Prang!* A high-pitched vibration travels through my skull, and I stagger back.

"Ho!" I say loudly, hoping to frighten Rudy into pulling his punches. "Hey, that really hurt," I whine, careful now to keep my voice low and to keep my back to Hector when I speak. Pain brings on a swift reinstatement of the double standard: *Yeah, I want to be treated just like one of the guys, except in the ring, except when I'm boxing a guy who's twice my weight.* Rudy smiles a little and he backs off, drops his fists, and opens his arms. This is as close to an outright insult as you can get in boxing, proof that you're not a true opponent.

I run at him full speed and let fly with my best combination: five punches in rapid succession, a jab, a hard right, a left uppercut to his jaw, a right cross, another jab. Nothing. I rapidly pound at his abdomen, left right, left right, on and on. Exhausted, I prance backward to catch my breath.

"Fight!" Hector yells, his usual command when I stop

punching. Rudy takes four big steps toward me and traps me in a corner. I duck my shoulder to him, turn, and bolt away along the ropes.

"Don' turn you back! Never turn you back!" I spin around again, and he's right there. The first punch lands on my ribs, just above my stomach. He's throwing a left, right, left, right combination, all to my body, gallantly, I suppose, avoiding my face. I'm now doubled over, eye level with the waistband of his trunks. I'm gasping out, "Stop! Stop!"

"You like it," he murmurs, as if we're playing some kind of sadistic sexual game.

"Please," I wheeze, tempted to collapse to the floor to emphasize the gravity of the situation. This sounds like the best plan, but when I try to fall, his punches are so rapid, they hold me up.

"Defense!" Hector hollers, but his voice is far away. I'm overwhelmed by fear and, yes, panic. Here it comes again. Frozen into a standing fetal position, I've forgotten what I'm supposed to do. Rudy changes his mind about avoiding my face; I'm in such a crouch that my head is the only target he can hit without kneeling down. A punch lands on my check, the mouthpiece saws into my gums. Roused by the temporary respite from body blows, I rise, bringing an uppercut with me. My fist meets his nostrils at the precise moment the bell rings.

I stagger over to Hector and spit out my mouthpiece before he can take it from me. The verbal abuse begins. I nod my head, too dazed to even listen. My ribs are killing me, and my arms are too heavy to lift. I open my mouth in a silent request for more water. As I drink, Hector holds the spit bucket; I demur and swallow. Not a practiced spitter, I'm afraid I won't hit the bucket, that I'll end up with spit drizzling down my chest. Opening my mouth for more, I receive instead my freshly rinsed mouthpiece.

The bell rings. "Move aroun'!" he commands. We touch gloves, and I start moving. Terrified, I bolt to all corners like a rabbit trapped in a cage with a bear. Rudy lumbers after me, like a big kid who wants to apologize for some accidental harm.

"You're good," he purrs as he blocks me into a corner. My eyes widen in alarm. These words, from another boxer, are usually the prelude to a real beating. "You hurt me, you know that?"

"You hurt me," I spit out, gasping for air, tripping briefly as my ankles collide in a desperate two-step dance away. "Stay the fuck away from me." I say this last part mostly to myself. We are, after all, in a boxing ring, and a part of me is fearful that he'll tell Hector that I'm afraid of him. Respecting an opponent is understood, acknowledging that they're superior is accepted, but stating that you're afraid of the person you're boxing is to denigrate the very essence of boxing: heart.

He dances in, my hands are raised up and braced, and I flinch. I have matchsticks for arms, and these are supposed to block his punches? I quickly throw a jab before he can break my forearm, and another, praying that it makes him, if only out of politeness, retreat. He stands firm.

"You wan' to stan', fight!" Hector yells. "Lef', right— use the jab!"

Rudy leans in and puts both of his forearms on my shoulders. I clutch tightly to him, grappling for purchase, trying to swing a punch into his kidneys. The weight of his body is causing my knees to buckle, and I'm audibly groaning with each exhalation. "What are we, dancing?" I growl. "You want to dance with me or fight me?" He pulls his right arm back, I duck his jab, and the bell rings.

Hector calls a halt to the proceedings, even though it's only been two rounds. I pretend to feel cheated.

"Hey," Rudy says, as we walk away, "you were good. Really. Some punches were hard. You hurt me, you know." Frowning, I gesture to let him know that his phony praise is an insult. He picks up his towel and carefully wipes down his face as we travel across the gym to the speed bags. He holds out the towel. Blood. A tiny smear.

"See? You clipped me! Your uppercut. It's dangerous. I mean it." I shake my head no, flushed with shame. He watched me drown on dry land, and now offers this crumb of praise to reassure me that while my performance was pretty horrible, I didn't humiliate myself entirely.

I finish my workout, my arms and legs trembling. Back in the locker room, I strip off my sodden unitard. The sharp ammonia tang brings on tears of self-pity, and then suddenly

I'm crying. I grab the roll of paper towels in my locker and press my face against it to muffle my sobs. *I was so scared out there!* I tell myself to let it out, it's just a natural reaction. In the next room, I can hear men joking, laughing, opening and closing lockers, flushing toilets. On this side of the wall, in the ladies' room, a sweaty, near-naked girl is clutching a roll of Bounty, shoulders heaving. *Pathetic.* What if someone came in right now? *Get a grip on yourself.*

When I get home, I take out Dr. Halpin's card and leave a message on his machine.

CALM, SHARP, ELUSIVE, VICIOUS

MIKE TYSON ENTERS the ring like a shark. He is an eating machine: indifferent, purposeful, unsentimental, cold. He has tiny eyes, a flat nose, and a head shaped like a bullet. His body is like a wall. In 1988, when Tyson was at his peak, it took 91 seconds for him to destroy the previously undefeated Michael Spinks. When asked how he pulled off such a stunning victory, Tyson said, "I saw the fear in his eyes." Spinks never boxed again.

The man who hypnotized the panic out of Mike Tyson is in my living room.

"You are never to be a standing target," intones Halpin. I'm seated in front of him on my sofa, in jeans and a T-shirt.

When Halpin returned my call, he suggested we have our session in my apartment. I'm uneasy about this strange man, credentials notwithstanding, who will be hypnotizing me in the privacy of my own home. And even as I doubt that I'll be able succumb to his commands, my worst fear is losing control. I call Eli and ask him to be here when the doctor comes, five days hence.

"The fundamentals!" Halpin emotes grandly. "You need to be calm, sharp, totally elusive, savage, and vicious. Being elusive isn't because you're afraid. You're repositioning for an attack. There are no negative emotions. *A killer capitalizes on his opponent's mistakes!*"

I wonder if Mike Tyson's concentration wanders with this man; he probably hears the same, platitude-laden speech. Is it possible that Tyson's violence has been unsheathed because of this hypnosis I'm about to experience? Am I about to be transformed into the same sort of rampaging, brutal thug? I guiltily acknowledge that part of me hopes that this gray-haired bespectacled man in his natty blue suit will bestow on me the ability to vanquish every opponent at Gleason's with a terrible fury. Visions of myself as the female Dirty Harry Callahan abound: "Go ahead. Make my day."

Dr. Halpin instructs me to place my hands on my knees in a relaxed manner. He tells me he'll do "the heavy lifting," but I'll perform maintenance on the hypnotic suggestions myself. From where I'm sitting, the object in front of me is the television, so my gaze is to be fixed, he says, on the word *Sony*, written on the bottom of the set. "Have you ever looked at a Magic Eye illustration?" he says. "The picture books where an image reveals itself only when you *relax* your gaze upon the picture?"

"Yes."

"This is the sort of *altered visual state of consciousness* you should be striving for. Stare at the word *Sony*. Blur it and clear it. Your eyelids are heavy." He continues on, asking me to relax my hands, to feel heavy, to "go to a wonderful place."

As he instructs me to slip away, I close my eyes. I can hear the leg of Eli's chair rumble briefly against the wooden floor. Will hearing the word *Sony* in future conversations turn me into a violent monster?

"You're not going to feel that fatigue," he says, referring to my earlier complaint that I often feel too tired in the ring to properly defend myself. "You're going to be calm, and sharp of mind. You'll be totally elusive, never presenting a frontal part of your body to an opponent. Always give angles! Use your jab." *A frontal part?* Is this why Mike Tyson uses such strange words at times? He starts to count from one to four. "You will feel great. Everything will be in effect."

Opening my eyes, I briefly wonder if I should mention that I was "awake" already. I'd hate to embarrass him.

Halpin tells me that he's about to give what's known as a "post-hypnotic suggestion." He stands and raises his arms away from his sides, until they're level with his shoulders. "Stand up," he says. "I want you to feel as if you have balloons on your wrists. Your arms are going to raise up from your sides—they're going to float up."

What a sham. *I'm* controlling my arms as they rise. The quicker I can get him out of here, the better. Tyson should have his head examined: first Don King, now this guy.

"The higher they go, the lighter they get," he says. "*Now.* Try to lower them."

Of course.

Then I try. I push down hard. So hard that my deltoids burn with the effort. Still, my arms stay where they are. I glance over at Eli and shake my head in wonder to let him know this is not an act. The hypnosis is actually working!

"I'm going to count to four," Dr. Halpin says, "and they'll stay locked until I say 'Okay.' " He pauses for extra drama. *"Okay!"* I lower my arms and feel a minor tremor in my shoulders from the exertion.

"But still they want to go up!" he cries again, and they rise without my help. "I want you to say 'I acknowledge all I see.' "

"I acknowledge all I see," I say, happily.

"Okay," he says with a wave of his hand, releasing my arms again. "You can sit back down." Eli claps his hands together softly in subdued applause.

Halpin explains that with a post-hypnotic suggestion, "The results will occur automatically. You should use all of these same commands to self-hypnotize yourself and reinforce the work we did today. Sit there, stare at the TV, relax your head, eyelids, arms, and legs. Give yourself permission. If you want to close your eyes on purpose, it's okay. Keep the conditioning short and sweet, say: 'I am calm, I am sharp, I am elusive, I am vicious.' Then count from one to four. Do it again," he says, adding, "if you like."

He watches me go through this little routine, and satisfied, he says, "You're on your way!"

The first person I'll spar with after being hypnotized is someone I've been mentally referring to as "the Little Dutch Boy." He started training with Hector a few weeks ago, and his flailing, spastic efforts on the speed bag have served to remind me just how far I've come. I heard he's an artist who lives in the area, but he's originally from Holland. Short, slight, and thin, with knobby, birdlike legs; even his head suggests a newly hatched sparrow, with a fine down of closely cropped blond hair and sharp unchanging features. Hector removes his small, round, wire-rimmed glasses just before sparring.

"You with heem," Hector says, pointing to my scrawny opponent, who is awkwardly jumping rope. This is hardly a fit test to see if I'm newly fearless. Still, I smile, anticipating an easy fight. Hector catches the meaning of my smile and laughs. Seeing our mutual glee, the gym cronies start shifting their seats to ringside in anticipation of an interesting battle. The subtle buzz in the gym isn't lost on the Little Dutch Boy.

"How long have you been training?" he says, as we step under the ropes. I ignore the question, as I silently chant "I am calm. I am sharp. I am elusive. I am vicious." Hector cups my chin to take my attention as he slides in the mouthpiece. "Jab, jab, get away from thees guy. Go in, go out. Make heem relax." I nod, but I'm thinking, *Relax, my ass.*

The bell rings. My opponent charges at me with the wide-eyed hysteria of full panic. I bite down hard on my mouthpiece, and without even touching gloves, we tear into each other, a blur of fists. The blows that connect feel like a hailstorm on my body; they have a sharp, high-pitched sound, as if he's rocketing them against a slab of aluminum. Individually they're unimpressive, but collectively they hurt. Half of them miss me entirely.

Part of me seems to be instructing my body from another room, my brain acting as a pilot busy at the controls of a 747. I'm as completely detached from emotional conflict as I would be playing a video game. Leaning into my punches harder than I ever have, all of my training coalesces; my hard right lands into the center of his face. His nose folds sideways under my glove, and this unexpected shifting of cartilage both sickens and excites me. Motion and sound slow to the point where I feel like I'm standing still in the silence, calmly studying the small veins bulging in his closed, fluttering eyelids, waiting for my left hook to make its way through the thickened air to arrive, stonelike, at his temple.

The noise roars back as time restarts itself, and despite his disorientation, he manages a glancing jab to my ribs. I can hear several people shouting "Don't hit so hard!" I throw one more light jab at his head as a parting threat and dance backward. He rushes into me again, nearly embracing me around the waist, and stabs at my kidneys. I smash an uppercut hard into his chin as he struggles upright. I can hear Hector saying "Stop! Stop!" over and over, but as far as I'm concerned, the Little Dutch Boy either goes down or the bell sounds—there's no possibility of me stopping. Hector leans into the ring and grabs him by the shoulder. He spins around, terrified. "Stop!" Hector screams into his face.

A trickle of blood is leaking out of his mouth. I feel guilty for not pulling my punches, but he asked for it, coming at me like a damned whirling dervish of flailing punches.

"I tol' you! *Don'—hit—so—hard!*" To my shock, this reprimand is being given to Dutch Boy, not me. "Go easy!" Hector commands him, as he rubs his shoulders, smiling and laughing a little at the boy's bravado. "Take it easy, ho-kay?" He slaps him on the back.

My opponent smiles sheepishly, unaware of the blood on his chin. He nods at Hector, and we square off again. "Fight!" Hector commands. I stare at my opponent warily and advance toward him slowly. He waits a moment and bursts out of the corner, resuming his wild swinging. A left slides off my headgear and into my left eye. I slam a right into his exposed torso and dance backward, ducking a roundhouse, my eye burning from the contact with leather. Tears cloud my vision momentarily. The chorus of disapproval is rising again, with Hector's voice in the forefront: "Hey! I tol' you don' hit so hard! *Hey!*"

Dutch Boy momentarily looks back to Hector, and Halpin's advice rings in my head: *A killer capitalizes on his opponent's mistakes.* Taking the golden opportunity, I slam a right into his exposed and unsuspecting jaw. He staggers sideways into the ropes, fury overtaking fear as his lips peel back from his clear plastic mouthpiece. I dance back for a second, unsure if I can attack a man on the ropes, but Hector is already waving his arms: *"STOP!"* The bell rings.

Hector yanks Dutch Boy backward out of the ring. Gigo unlaces his gloves so there can be no misunderstanding. Hector climbs into the ring and shakes his head apologetically. "You no fight him. He too scared, act crazy!" He plucks out my mouthpiece and places it in its orange plastic case, then calls out in Spanish for his mitts. Dutch Boy is sent off with a punching bag to cool off on the other side of the room. The spectators break apart and go back to their usual spots against the wall. A few look over, smiling and nodding appreciatively. I raise my glove in acknowledgment. Gigo smiles at me: a first.

The bell rings, and Hector holds up the mitts. "Wan,

two," he says. Jab, right. "Wan, two," he says again. Jab, right. "Hard!" he says. Bam, *bam*.

He smiles and lets out a laugh. "You hit," he says, "like *an animal*." I resist the instinct to smile back. I maintain my position, hard, stern, ready for war. I am calm, sharp, elusive, and I am vicious.

THE GIRL

BRUCE IS SITTING in his office, behind his vast un-
cluttered desk, studying the screen of his laptop. I've just
handed him $50, which he has tucked into his front pants
pocket, after fishing out $5 for me as change. I'm paying
my dues for the upcoming month, so he's fooling with the
mouse, scrolling around, noting the forty-five-dollar cash
transaction in the computer. "You interested in scheduling
a fight?" he says, still staring at the screen. For the past
month, I've been telling Bruce that I'd like to enter some
sort of boxing event.

"You mean a real fight?" I ask him, making sure he's not just talking about a sparring partner for the afternoon. "Where I get to box a woman? One who's actually in my weight class?"

"Oh, yes," he says, looking up. "We're going to sponsor a night of boxing, and we'll have boxers from all over coming in. I just have to match everyone up, see if I can get the proper opponents. Are you interested?"

"Sure! When?"

"In, oh, I don't know," he says, wearily rubbing one eye, "about . . . two months. I'll let you know for sure if I can find someone for you. Sometime in early November, I think."

"Fine. Count me in." *Two months.* A flush of blood travels down my body, starting at my face, which is hot. Goose bumps break out on my arms. *A real fight.* Eight weeks.

"How much do you weigh?" he says, writing my name down in a small notebook.

"One twenty-seven, one thirty. Something like that. Last I checked."

"Junior lightweight," he says, making another notation. I walk out to find Hector. He's playing dominos in his office with Gigo and is already smiling when I walk in. He must be winning. I'll tell him what I just heard.

"Ha! We kick butt!" he says.

"Maybe I should spar with a woman sometime. I've never done that." The few women I've seen at Gleason's only get in the ring with their trainers. "I should probably get used to it, you know, before the fight. To see what it's like." His smile disappears. Does he understand me? "Someone who's more—my weight, my experience. Just to see where I am with all that." I shift my weight from one foot to the other, lean forward a bit, and raise my eyebrows; the usual cues for your conversational partner that it's his turn to speak.

"What you standin' there for?" Hector says, raising his arms impatiently. "Get dress!"

Two weeks later, Hector tells me he's set me up with a female sparring partner for the following Saturday. My mouth goes completely dry. I asked for it, but now I'm not sure if this is good news or bad. Until now, my concern has been to do well against opponents who are far more experienced than I am, who are stronger, taller, heavier, the Little Dutch Boy notwithstanding. I remember the Golden Gloves fights I saw last February, and the way the women ran out of their corners flailing and thrashing at each other like fighting cocks; a blurred hysteria of violence. Maybe I'm actually safer boxing men.

"Who is she?" Please let it not be that hulking, sullen heavyweight teenager.

"I train her before. She cryin' to Bruce, say I'm too tough." He laughs in that special, high-pitched way he reserves for mocking cowards.

To my surprise, I can hardly sleep on Friday night. This is preposterous. After everything I've gone through, is it possible I'm actually scared to fight a woman? She's not the one who's been boxing men three times a week for the past ten months. She thought Hector was too tough, and here am I: calm, sharp, elusive, vicious. Maybe I'm not afraid of *her*, maybe I'm afraid of *me*. I'm going to really hurt someone tomorrow. Someone who's just like me.

No, a more likely fear is this: What if—after ten months of fighting, preparation, hypnosis, and all the rest of it— this girl, this coward who thinks Hector is a scary bad man, takes me apart, pummels me, knocks me down? I might as well quit and never come back. Now I can find out exactly how good or bad I really am.

At Gleason's, I walk into an empty gym. Hector is alone, standing by the front door. "Where is everybody? Is it open?"

"She's in the locker room."

Bruce is in his office and waves as I pass by. There's one man shadowboxing against the mirror near the ladies' room. I guess Saturday mornings aren't popular for boxing. Good, no audience.

I burst through the door of the locker room, and the only woman inside freezes at the sight of me. She has a locker door open, one two doors away from mine. She's a little shorter than I am, with a more petite build, but there's sinewy muscle definition in her arms. She's wearing a sleeveless T-shirt and tight Lycra shorts; her hair is cropped short and dyed blond, with about an inch of darker roots showing through the tousled spikes. This bright youthful hairstyle makes for a stark contrast to a face that looks far older, with cobwebs of wrinkles around each eye and tiny lines on her upper lip: the hallmark of a longtime smoker. Her face doesn't look aged as much as weathered, and what speaks the loudest of a hard past is the tattoo on her cheekbone, a small star. A gang sign?

"Hi," I say. "Sorry I'm a little late."

"That's okay! I just got here." Her voice is breathless, nervous, much softer than her face.

"I'm Lynn."

"Darla." We shake hands awkwardly. Her hand is small and cool, a gentle grasp. "I didn't want to do this," she says. She sounds like a Long Island girl. Or Jersey. Something local. "But Hector, he insisted. I mean, I don't want to get hurt, I'm scared." I'm so surprised that she's as anxious as I am that I almost burst out laughing.

"Look, I don't want to get hurt either," I say, opening my locker. "I've been a little—" I search for the word. What is the word? "Nervous—about this too."

"Can we just say we won't hit each other very hard?" she says. I stop unbuttoning my pants for a moment. *Fixed fight* floats to mind. She taps me on the shoulder, indicating that I should face her. "Like this. Can I just hit you to show you? I'll hit you here, in your shoulder." Her arm snakes slowly through the air, and her fist lands into my shoulder with gradually applied pressure. A playful punch from a friend has hurt me more. "Did that hurt?"

"Come on, you can hit harder than that. I mean, that was ridiculous. I don't think Hector would quite buy it."

Standing here waiting for her to hit me again, I expect to feel relief, but instead I'm let down, deflated, disappointed. I was all set to meet success or failure head-on. She bats at me with more conviction. "I won't ever hit you harder than that, okay?"

"Okay, now me," I tell her. I can't believe I feel sorry enough for this woman to throw this fight. I had never considered the possibility that instead of fear, I'd feel pity. I slug at her shoulder. "How's that?"

"Good. That's fine."

"I won't hit you in the face," she says as I turn back to my locker, and it's clear I'm expected to reciprocate.

"Okay, I won't hit you in the face." A moment later I add, "Just body shots." She should understand that I'll feel obligated to hit her *somewhere*.

"Great!" She hops up once, a feminine gesture of glee. "God, I feel so much better, I'm so glad you feel this way too." *Feel this way too?* That she sees us as being the same gives me a slight stab of regret. While I'm uneasy about accepting the offer of a fixed fight—but that uneasiness sure didn't stop me from accepting it—I know that even in my darkest hour last night, the thought of asking for a fix never occurred to me. I cling to this thin shred of evidence of my superior character as I tug on my Everlast shorts. I mean, this is practically entrapment. I never would have arranged this on my own. I'm just being polite. Christ, she's scared enough as it is—what am I supposed to do, tell her "Forget it, I'm going to beat the tar out of you, too damned bad if you don't want to get hurt"?

"I'll wait for you," she says, sliding down the wall to a sitting position on the ratty carpet. "I don't want to go out there alone."

Having her near me is suddenly annoying. Even her presence is a responsibility: she doesn't want to go out there by herself. I dress as quickly as possible, grab my gear, and walk out ahead of her, to cut conversation to a minimum. I grab a jump rope and look around for Hector, who is nowhere in sight. Darla occupies herself with her equipment while I lightly skip.

One round passes, and Hector emerges from the men's locker room. Wordlessly taking my jump rope out of my hands as he walks by, he finds my gloves and fishes the neatly rolled wraps out of them. Waving me over and taking my hands, he leans in, his voice low. "Go in, go out, hit her in the face, hit her in the body. She won' know what to do."

Two men walk in, a couple of the regular spectators; retirees content to sit on a bench and converse about the boxers in Spanish all day long. They wave at Hector. And now that they see two women in headgear, the newspapers they brought in with them are folded and tucked away, and they select two folding chairs to drag over to our ring. Two women boxing is a novelty act, something different, and something sexual as well; they settle in amid much leering and elbowing. *Ringside at a catfight.*

It's odd to see such a small opponent in the opposite

corner. Darla's eyes are enormous behind glossy red head-gear that looks fresh out of the box. I nod at her, a signal to calm down. I'd smile, but I don't want Hector to get too suspicious. The bell rings; a metal chair squeaks in eager anticipation.

We touch gloves, and she backs away, fists raised. Cautiously, I throw a slow right to her left shoulder. She taps me in reply, using the same punch. "Fight!" Hector yells. I dance backward and let her chase me for a little while, dodging her slow swipes. "Come on!" Hector is screaming. "Fight! Jab, jab! Fight! Use you fists!" A glance into her eyes to allow her to get ready, and then I let off a flurry of light blows to her ribs. She fights back with a right to my chest, but it skids off and clips me in the jaw. It doesn't hurt in the least, but she looks horrified, as if she's about to blurt out an apology. Hector's rants have melded into one angry chant: "Fight, fight, fight! Why you no' fighting!" We go on like this for three minutes in a parody of boxing, a clumsy, mocking ballet.

The bell rings. Hector is furious, facing the two of us. "You better fight. *I heard you in there!*" My stomach clenches as he glares at each of us in turn, pointing at the locker rooms. The men's room. The partition. He walked in there right after I entered the women's room and overheard every word. I look over at Darla to see if she's bothering to deny this accusation. Her mouth shut, head down, she's pleading guilty. Dizzy with the gut-wrenching anxiety of being caught, I can be grateful for two things. One, he must know it was her idea. The other, that I didn't complain about Hector's harassment and my recent troubles with him. Staring down at my sneakers, I try to look repentant. "Right now," Hector says, shaking his finger at us, "you fight!" For a moment, I'm torn between giving my word and obeying Hector. He glares at me murderously. Okay, to hell with her.

We hear the signal for round two. Right after we touch gloves, I smash her in the ribs, but I figure she understands. Like some of the kindhearted brutes I've fought, I decide to spare her any head shots and focus instead on blows to her body.

When my glove makes contact with her ribs, an image of a bird's nest comes to mind; a mass of strong but tiny twigs and branches. Hitting a man in the side is usually like striking vulcanized rubber: resilient, hard, impervious. But she's all angles and points, a creature made out of wire and wood. Scared, she's lashing out at my head, completely ignoring my body. Her punches originate from her shoulders, and there's little behind them other than the velocity of her arm.

Dancing back and exhaling to clear my head from the clanging of her punches, I come in to her to practice defense. She backs away at first, then advances with her jab. Stepping aside, I'm stunned that it didn't graze me anywhere; it's the first punch I've ever dodged so precisely. Turning around to her again, like a matador to a bull, I ready myself for her next charge: another punch to the head, no doubt.

I'm not wrong. We dance around like this for another minute, until Hector starts yelling for blood: hers. "Fight! Hit! Hit!" Coming in fast, I lean into my right for a shot to her ribs, then a left, another left, another right. She's going limp against my fists. A lightbulb clicks on inside my skull: *These body blows really work!* They take the spark out of everyone, not just me. The power to drain the life out of her is intoxicating; I'm fighting an urge to giggle with delight. One of the old guys watching is yelling something in Spanish, urging us on, demanding more. Darla leans against me for a moment, and without thinking, my female, ever-helpful reflex is to hold her up, as if we're exhausted marathon dancers.

"What you doing!" says Hector, his voice rising an octave. "Fight!" She leaps away as from a hot stove. She comes in with a surprising right and knocks me hard in the cheekbone. Dazed for a moment, I advance and we grapple in a clinch, a mad embrace. *Her hair smells nice. Coconutty.* The bell rings. Hector is braying with laughter.

"Ha-ha! Good!" He removes my mouthpiece and wipes down my sweaty face with a towel. After giving me a drink, he walks over to Darla and offers her the same. "You doing good," I hear him tell her. "Defen' youself."

I had expected the hypnosis to act as a numbing drug, but what it does is siphon off the paralyzing fear and panic attacks that interfere with rational thought. Once in the ring, I can still feel anxious over whether I'll do well, whether I can protect myself effectively, but the irrational fears—that I can't get enough air, that I'll die if I don't run away—are thankfully gone.

The bell rings, and we touch gloves. Darla's eyes have lost that open, swimming look; they've narrowed, and her features are grimly set, the gates down and locked. No longer scared; she's angry. This transition has, up until now, been my exclusive experience.

To the novice, facing a new opponent in round one is pure performance anxiety, which is tiring in and of itself, as worrying about anything is incredibly exhausting. Round two is far worse, as real physical fatigue combines with the twin fears of injury and imminent exhaustion, a crazy, self-firing circuit of slow suffocation. But sometimes the gods smile, and round three is magically fueled by righteous anger. It's possible for fear to be crowded out by the indignation that rises out of being picked on and terrorized for two rounds. On those rare occasions, I have felt as if a switch has flipped: fear to violence. Six minutes is, occasionally, blessedly, the cutoff for being flat-out scared. It's as if my brain decides it can't tolerate the overload of adrenaline and the blinding haze of hysteria, and so a rerouting of emotion takes place. Anger brings a lust for revenge, and with it, a second wind.

Darla is furious about the stabs to the ribs. She punches my gloves at the start of the round and starts swinging. I jab at her shoulders and keep back, knowing that this sort of fighting burns out after about thirty seconds. She backs away, breathing hard, her white mouthpiece visible in a grimace. *Now.* Advancing with regret at the prospect of having to expend my own dwindling energy, I start a volley of body blows and combined defense, batting down her arms as they venture up to my head, still her only target. Was this what it was like for Jesse, fighting me when I never threw another kind of punch? The thirty-second warning bell for the end of the round sounds, and we enter into full-on, fighting-cock territory: flailing, thrashing, pushing.

The buzzer finally sounds, and we stop. Two spectators are applauding; Hector is laughing and nodding at them. "Good job," I tell Darla, giving her a brief hug.

"Yeah!" she says with the enthusiasm of relief. "You too. Good job!" Inexperienced with speaking with a mouthguard in, her speech has the dull consonants of the hearing-impaired.

Hector unfastens my headgear and takes out my mouthguard. "Tha's it! Get dress!" he says, quickly unlacing my gloves.

Back in the locker room, we strip down in near silence. We point and make faces as if to caution each other about the possibility of being monitored from the next room, but there's nothing much to say anyhow. She's happy she's not hurt, I'm happy I did well.

"Hey," she says, as we both clang our lockers shut and prepare to leave, "be careful."

"I will," I tell her, surprised and a little embarrassed. This seemed like such a hollow victory. "Thanks."

Walking out into the gym, Hector is standing with the retirees, who look over at us, beaming. "She kick you ass!" Hector yells at Darla. "She kick you ass!" Darla turns and walks into Bruce's office, giving a small wave of acknowledgment toward this unseemly display, her face grim. Hanging back, I pretend that I need something deep in the pockets of my handbag to allow Darla time to get inside Bruce's office before I reach Hector. Finally pulling out my datebook as if this were the errant object of my search, I continue my walk toward the men.

"Hey!" Hector says, and I smile back. "Why you let her tell you not to hit!"

"Oh that," I say, wishing he would let the whole thing die already. "She seemed so scared, what could I do?"

"What you do? You hit her!" A brief flash of anger. "Tha's what you do!"

"Next time, sure." Realizing I'm still holding my datebook, I open it as if I have to write in our next appointment. "Monday? Same time?"

"Yes, you come in Monday," he says impatiently. As if I could forget: Monday, Wednesday, and Friday mornings are all I think about—my entire career and social life are scheduled around these several hours. But I'm holding my book, so I write it in. Snapping it shut and dropping it in my bag, I extend my hand.

"Thanks," I say as he shakes it and then lifts it to his

mouth for a loud kiss on my bruised knuckles. The retirees hoot as he smiles lasciviously. Tugging my hand back, I slap him lightly on his biceps and roll my eyes in exasperation. The retirees continue their laughing and chattering in Spanish.

Walking down the stairs, I wipe my hand on my blue jeans and check my watch. I hold it to my ear for a moment, to make sure it's working: since I entered Gleason's this morning, I've experienced anxiety, empathy, shame, exhilaration, and triumph. Only thirty minutes have passed.

THE WHITE GUY PROBLEM

IN RETROSPECT, ONE of the reasons my marriage eventually failed was that my husband couldn't wholly accept that I had changed. When we met I was eighteen and still in college and he was twenty-three with a car, his own apartment, and, most important to him, an all-consuming job as a successful set designer—first in the theater, and then in film and television. During the twelve years we lived together, his work ethic helped me transform myself from a needy party girl into an independent career woman. While that transformation seemed to be something he

216

encouraged, in reality, he was threatened by it. That my in-
dependence gave him more pain than joy made me angry.
After nearly a year that rage had only intensified—and was
unfortunately unleashed upon a man who happened to
walk into Gleason's one day with his young son.

The man is in his late thirties, with the prosperous appearance of a banker on his day off. His tanned skin con-
trasts with a tousled shock of prematurely gray hair, and a
gold wedding band gleams on his left hand. He's dressed in
a pale blue button-down shirt and khaki pants with pleats
in the front, well-worn and perfectly broken-in leather
loafers, no socks. His son shares the same square face and
full mouth as his father. The boy looks to be nine or ten
years old and sports a Nike T-shirt and new-looking blue
jeans, the cuffs draping heavily against his Timberland
boots. The father is observing the scene at Gleason's with a
browser's curiosity, as if he's entering a shop he'd read
about in a travel magazine.

I'm skipping rope when I see this small family unit, and
my stomach tightens reflexively. I know he's going to approach me—I'm white, and I'm a woman.

Gilbert is baby-sitting Hector's boxers today because
Hector and Gigo are in Belgium.

"Who's fighting over there?" I ask, hanging up the rope.

"Not sure," says Gilbert, watching me shadowbox. The
boy and his father have walked into Bruce's office. *He's not
here because he thinks his kid should learn how to fight, is
he?* That's like something Hemingway or Norman Mailer

would do; drag his son over to some rough gym, as if getting the crap beaten out of him, and learning how to beat the crap out of someone, will teach him about being a man.

"Such horseshit," I murmur.

"No, I don't know," Gilbert says, still on Belgium. "If I knew I'd say."

"No, forget it, I don't care." It's too complicated to explain, and so I continue my warm-up in silence. Three rounds later, it's time to lace up.

"You spar with Eric. You fight him before? It's okay?" Gilbert still feels responsible for the pounding I suffered with Dominick.

"Yeah, I fight him all the time. He's good, I'll be fine." And calm, sharp, elusive, vicious.

Eric and I are well into our second round together when this man and his son materialize next to our ring. I've been doing well, and Eric, having long abandoned the notion that he shouldn't hit me hard, has landed some solid punches, smiling bashfully when he knows he got in a good one.

Eric steps to my left and drops his left hand at the same time. I take the opening and throw a hard right to his jaw. His head snaps to the side, and he shakes it in surprise. I smile back. I have no fear anymore; sparring is like playing a video game, although the mistakes made are still painful. Then a voice cuts through our silent workout.

"Use your right."

Quickly cutting my eyes in the direction of the command, I see Mr. J. Crew and Son.

"Miss. Use your right!"

Deliberately jabbing with my left, I step too far forward, and Eric locks me into a brief clinch. Using the moment to relax my arms for a second and catch my breath, we shove apart, and I throw a right hook.

"Use your right. Miss! Throw a right! A right!"

I make a face to Eric as if to say "Can you believe this guy?" Chewing down hard on my mouthpiece, *calm, sharp, elusive, vicious,* I practice a combination: jab, right, uppercut.

"Miss!" His voice is louder now, more urgent. "Miss, use your right!" He thinks he's helping me. He thinks he's welcome. His presumption is over the line. I raise a glove to Eric to request a break in the action. He drops his arms.

Turning, I stride quickly over to where the father and son are standing. His head just clears over the top of the ropes, and he has an expectant look on his face, pleased, interested. His son looks nervous, worried.

"You're telling me I should use my right."

"Yes," he says.

Months ago, I would have told him off. Now I simply act.

I throw my right hard into his face. The punch lands mostly onto his cheekbone, which is fleshier than I had expected. It's like punching an expensive, modern couch and feeling the stuffing behind the sleek upholstery. His head jerks back for a second, but other than that, he's too shocked to move. His face crumples a bit; he looks horribly wounded, not all of it physical.

"Like that, you mean?" He stares as I speak; saddened, disappointed, shocked, and, it seems, betrayed. He's still holding his son's hand. "Look," I continue, "don't tell me what to do. It's very *distracting*." Any word with an S in it is difficult to enunciate properly with a mouthguard, so I say it slowly, so he's sure to understand me. I look over at the ring just behind him, where two middleweights are sparring, their bodies sleek with sweat, muscles rippling as they grapple in a clinch. "Why don't you go over there, and tell *them* what to do."

The guy still hasn't spoken or moved. I glance at his son, who's staring at me wide-eyed, as if I live in his bedroom closet. *Suddenly it dawns on me. I shouldn't have hit him in front of his son.* I bound back over to Eric, who's giggling in his silent, shaking-shoulders way.

"Was that bad, what I just did?" I ask him in a worried voice as we touch gloves again. He pulls his arms into a boxing stance and, grinning, shakes his head no. "Would you have done that?" A vigorous nod yes. Relieved, I smile back and throw a jab, which misses him by a mile. Maybe I taught the kid a couple of good life lessons: When you're a stranger in a strange land, you're better off keeping your suggestions to yourself, and never tell a woman what to do if she happens to be wearing boxing gloves.

THE QUARTER

THE TRADITIONAL METHOD of training for an athletic event, whether it's a marathon or a prizefight, is to
gradually increase the intensity and duration of workouts
so that the event lands at a point when strength and endurance are at their highest. To try to maintain that level
for weeks and months is a process of diminishing returns:
the body will break down under the strain of high maintenance. Hector should have backed me off my training for a
few weeks after the fight was announced, then taken it up
to the point we are now. There is a look of strength that is

robust and carefully built, and then there is what I have—the meager power that comes out of desperation and necessity, the musculature of the laborer in an internment camp. I looked frayed, a rope that's starting to tear.

There's a full-length mirror on the bedroom side of my bathroom door. Sunlight streams through a nearby window in the morning, and it's here that I get dressed and study, for better and worse, my changing body. Months ago I had imagined that boxing would put me in the very best shape of my life, that I'd emerge from the training as a lean, mean fighting machine. The reality is different.

My feet are ruined. Bruised and missing toenails aside, I remain hopeful that they will someday, somehow, shrink back to my pre-Marathon size eight. A year of running followed by a year of boxing has meant that I have a closet full of shoes I can't wear for more than a few agonizing hours. For the past year, I've been making do with three pairs of shoes in nine or nine and a half, reluctant to buy more in case my feet shrink or my tolerance for tight shoes rises. Another year will pass before I'll admit that I'm at least a size nine and give all of my other shoes to the Salvation Army.

My legs are more muscled than they were eight months ago; my quads are thicker, my hamstrings bow out when viewed from the side, and my calves have swelled. Those chic black-patent-leather knee-high boots I bought two years ago are impossible to zip up.

My abdomen seems wider than it has a right to be; my waist isn't narrow anymore, it's flat, strong, and broad. The biggest surprise is my upper body. My pectorals are fleshy, and my back flares out dramatically up to my shoulders. Just last week I sneezed at my desk while wearing a scarf-thin beige silk top, and it promptly ripped open at the back, near the left underarm seam. Flexing my arms, I can make my biceps pop out impressively, but then I see my neck. It's a quarter of an inch bigger in circumference, and my trapezius muscles angle more sharply into my shoulders. They used to be nearly straight across, and now it's as if flesh, like packed wet sand, has been ever-so-slightly built up to buttress my vulnerable neck. A linebacker neck.

My hands are larger and broader, each finger is bigger, and no matter how much I ice them, my knuckles won't go back down. An opal ring that used to belong to my great-grandmother will never fit again.

I don't see a strong, lean, and mean fighting machine in the mirror, ready to do battle in less than a month. I see an overtrained boxer, a car whose engine has been revved beyond the red line for months, and smoke is starting to escape from beneath its well-polished hood.

I have twelve more boxing workouts, forty-eight rounds of sparring, sixty miles of running, eight hours of weight lifting, and just four days of rest before the big day.

———

Reggie Tuur is a flashy, ambitious boxer who knows the value of a strong personality when it comes to endorsement deals. He stops hitting the heavy bag when he sees me come in, then nods and smiles. I offer a quick wave as I pass, preoccupied with prefight fretting. Coming out of the locker room, I'm surprised to hear him call me by name. He's pulled his gloves off.

"Lynn," he says, holding up a quarter. "Try." He gestures for me to stand opposite him. "Put that down," he says, talking about my headgear and my gloves and wraps. "You hold this," he says, placing the coin into my outstretched hand. "I stand over here." He backs an arm's length away from my palm and gets into a boxer's stance. "When you see my arm move"—he throws a jab, reaching toward my palm and the quarter—"you close your hand. Stop me from getting the coin. You try to be faster than my jab. Like this," he says, demonstrating my part, arm straight, palm up, fingers slamming shut over the coin in one quick movement.

"Okay," I say, intrigued by the idea of this quick-draw contest.

We position ourselves. I practice closing my fist around the coin a couple of times and nod okay. The round bell sounds, and a few boxers turn to watch during the lull.

"Three," he intones, "two . . . you ready? Okay. Two . . . one." His hand flies out toward mine, and my fist clamps down as if I'm capturing a fly. I'm afraid to unfold my fingers in case the quarter will fly out somehow.

Reggie is facing me, smiling. He reaches into the fist of his left hand and removes the quarter. Amazed, I open my hand. Nothing.

"Again," he says, handing me the quarter. Firmly pressing it into my palm, I extend my fingers and watch him carefully. He counts down.

"Three . . . two . . . one." A blur flashes in front of me, and my fist curls fast against the coin. Safe!

Reggie holds up the quarter.

"How . . . ?" I say, bewildered. I never felt the brush of his fingers. Is it a magic trick, where he has extra quarters in his hand? But how does he make my quarter disappear? "Wait, one more time."

"Okay, but now I don't count. You just watch me."

"Let's go." I stare at him, eyes open wide, ready to take in everything. His arm moves, my fist closes. He laughs. I don't even have to open my hand. I know the quarter's gone. A few boxers chuckle and turn back to their workouts; the round bell has sounded again.

"Jesus!" I say, impressed. "You are fast. That's really cool. How do you do it?"

"I'm fast," he says with a wink, taking back the quarter.

I once read that the very best athletes see faster than the rest of us. The athletes themselves are rarely able to describe exactly what makes them stand above the thousands of very good players, but occasionally, when pressed, it seems to be about their ability to take in and process more details during a game. "To me," said hockey superstar Wayne Gretzky, "it's like everything is happening in slow motion." On the ice, Gretzky had a particular genius for anticipation. Most offensive players want the action behind them, making scoring a battle between themselves and the goalie. Gretzky kept it in front, somehow seeing a thousand different indicators about where the puck would wind up, and then, a second later, being at the exact spot to grab it when it arrived.

Basketball great Michael Jordan habitually processed thousands of possibilities for scoring during a play, before intuiting exactly when and where and how he should position and move himself to make a basket. Our perception is that he did this in a linear fashion, methodically considering and discarding each option, like the ticking of a stopwatch. If that were the case, Jordan would be the human equivalent of Deep Blue, the chess computer able to whiz through every possible permutation of an opponent's next move and countermove. Jordan didn't do this—his method of determining and discarding game plans happened by processing information simultaneously. The way he sees can be better described as a gestalt: to see everything at once, rather than as individual pieces of information.

A so-called "idiot savant," an autistic who is also, somehow, a math genius, such as the one portrayed by Dustin

Hoffman in the film *Rain Man*, approaches numbers in much the same way. There is a scene in the film where a waitress drops a large box of toothpicks, and with one glance, Hoffman's character correctly tells her how many are lying in a heap on the floor. This is astounding to the rest of us, because we count objects one at a time. This ability may come from a unique way of seeing the whole, of counting all of the toothpicks at once. The ability to calculate the square root of an eleven-digit number comes not from working through a dozen complicated steps, but from seeing the numbers in their totality; from seeing the woods, and not being distracted by all of the trees.

Psychologists describe this way of thinking as "chunking." The reason chess masters can view a game in progress for a few seconds and then reconstruct the pieces on a different board is because they break the board down into large, familiar chunks: two or three groups of chess pieces in positions they have seen many times before. Gretzky, like Jordan, didn't see eleven players individually—he was seeing familiar groupings, and from that, he could extrapolate what would happen from each chunk because he'd witnessed it before. Even though boxers are facing only one opponent, I wonder if this theory could also be valid for their ability to correctly anticipate: experienced fighters have encountered the same postures, the same subtle body language over and over. They might "see" punches through the chunking of the many indicators that precede it, the tilt of the head and hips, a shift in the shoulders, the angle of a glove. By the time the fist is in the air, it's usually too late to avoid it.

Reggie's mysterious trick with the quarter preys on my mind. Perhaps its success hinges not on his speed, but on my ability to watch him move.

I see Tuur again one week later. He's walking in just as I'm hanging up a jump rope at the end of my workout. Hector is sitting nearby in a chair, next to the equipment locker.

"You have a quarter?" I ask him. Pleased, he digs in his pockets.

"You want to see it disappear again," he says, grinning at Hector and putting his gym bag down on the floor. He takes off his zippered jacket and unbuttons the cuffs on his shirt, carefully rolling them up his thick forearms. He winks and squeezes my hand as he gives me the quarter.

Standing the requisite distance away, I empty my mind and focus on the entire area that Tuur occupies before me. Willing myself not to wait and watch for his approaching hand, I want to simply feel when he's going to jab. We wait a few seconds, my palm stretches out between us. Suddenly, like a cobra strike, his arm is out and back. Reggie opens his palm with a smile, but—no quarter.

I open my hand, and there it is, winking in the glare of fluorescent light. "Let's do it again."

This time Tuur narrows his eyes as he faces me and waits several seconds before moving, hoping the suspense and anticipation will put me off balance. I think of the whole, his entire body. I don't know what I'm looking for, but I know my brain has already seen it many, many times.

His arm darts toward me. Was I too late? I uncurl my fingers: the quarter is mine.

THE PARTY

ELI AND HIS two roommates, a struggling stand-up co-
median and a junior executive on Wall Street, are throwing
a party. Weeks earlier they discussed this proposed event
with their neighbor, an aspiring graphics designer, who
shares their hallway in a dingy, fifth-floor walk-up in
Chelsea. He suggests expanding the festivities to include
his place and his friends as well. The idea is to open both
apartments, and let the parties, and their diverse guests,
commingle. It's a crowded, rowdy, sprawling affair, with
people filling every room, every sitting surface, spilling out

into the hall, the staircase, on up to the rooftop. While the guests may believe they're vastly different from one another for one reason or another, to me they seem mostly the same. All still in their early to mid-twenties, they're recent college graduates just venturing out into the world.

Dressed for the occasion in a black stretch miniskirt, black tights, and a tight, bright orange T-shirt that says A CLOCKWORK ORANGE, the logo from the Kubrick film, I've abandoned the idea of finding anything to drink other than beer, so I'm sipping from a bottle of Miller Lite. I have on new shoes: oversized black-patent-leather lace-ups, a cartoonlike parody of normal footwear. On the walk over to the party, a bike messenger spied them and shouted, "Hey, Sasquatch," as he passed. They're heavy but comfortable and roomy inside, perfect for my tender toenails.

Eli's two brothers are also in attendance, one older, Adam, and one younger, Gabriel. The three brothers are each a symmetrical two years apart, but the maturity level is reversed: the youngest is the most grounded and responsible, and the eldest is a well-meaning goof. Eli's entire family, including the parents, regard me as if I'm a rare and mythical woodland creature who's wandered into their midst: an older divorcée who takes their son/brother to interesting events, restaurants, and parties. They're pleased and excited and take lots of pictures, but it's as if they know he and I do not have a real future together.

Eli is sitting on the stairs leading to the roof. I've staked out a spot nearby, in the hallway between the two apartments, and am talking to one of Eli's old friends, Brad, who's come down from Boston just for this occasion. Brad's from a wealthy family but is still "finding himself" while living at home.

"Probert," he says out of the blue. Probert is the name of a hockey player renowned for his violent tendencies. "This guy can't skate onto the ice without the crowd shouting 'Goon! Goooon!' over and over. He fights constantly. It's what he does."

"Fascinating," I tell him.

Just then Eli's brother Adam bounds over to us and playfully shoves me in the arm.

"Wanna fight?" he says, his face flushing pink. Adam laughs a little too hard at this question, as if it's the wittiest thing he's ever heard himself say.

"That's okay, Adam," I tell him with a patient smile.

"Come on! Fight me!" he says, wriggling around like a kid overdue for the bathroom. "Bet you can't!"

"Adam," Eli calls out, "stop being an asshole." I glance over to Eli on my left, and *thonk*! To my astonishment, Adam has hit me, although not very hard, in the right side of my jaw. There's a dime-sized ache where his knuckles rapped against my jawbone.

"*Sucker* punch!" I blurt out, appalled, and shove my beer into Brad's hand. Adam has bounded down the stairs, two at a time, his laughter following his descent.

"Don't run, Adam!" Eli yells down. "She *hates* cowards!" I take two steps down the stairs after him and stop.

My new shoes are too big and clunky to navigate steps efficiently.

"Adam!" I yell down. "Come back up here, you coward!" I stomp back up to my spot in the hallway. "Jesus, he
sucker punched me!" I announce to the small group of
gawkers. Adam's laughter, now at a higher pitch, floats up
the stairs. "Learn to fight like a man!" I yell back.

Retrieving my beer from Brad, I apologize for leaving
our conversation so abruptly.

Eli brushes past us and asks if we need anything from
the kitchen. I shake my head, holding up the same bottle of
beer I've been nursing for an hour. Adam's girlfriend, Lisa,
takes Eli's spot on the staircase and waves at us.

"Your boyfriend is being an asshole," Eli calls out to
her, loud enough for Adam to hear, but he'll probably inter-
pret that comment as a compliment, as in, "He's an amus-
ing asshole, and that's why we love him so." She smiles
back and rolls her eyes in sympathy.

"So anyway," Brad says, "Probert is just as bad off the
ice." He elaborates, telling stories of substance abuse, but
when I look over his shoulder, I see Adam slinking up the
stairs. *Calm, sharp, elusive, vicious.* Adam sees me watching him and giggles mischievously, the practiced, self-
conscious laugh of a guy who thinks he's being cute. I remain
motionless and look back at Brad, as if I can't tear myself
away. Something within me is struggling to come out; I feel
the beating of wings against the bars of my rib cage. *Come
on, Adam. Just a few more steps, and I can block your*

escape route. ". . . so I have this videotape of all his best fights," drones Brad. "Players are actually physically afraid of him! I love this guy, he's a total maniac."

"Hold my beer," I say, smiling. Adam has moved away from the stairs and is now chatting with another couple.

"All right," Brad says awkwardly.

My hands now free, I take two swift steps to the head of the stairs and reach out with my right arm to yank Adam around to me by his left shoulder. Spinning around, Adam's nose makes brief and brutal contact with my left jab. Exhilarated by this perfect violent moment, my right follows immediately to his entirely unprotected ribs. Strange to fight without gloves. My arms feel too light, my fists too vulnerable. There's a moist spot on my left knuckle: Adam's snot? Disgusting. Gloves protect in more ways than one.

"Hey!" he yells, in pain, but on some level, almost happy for the attention. I shove him with both hands, and he takes a step backward into a woman who squeals in protest, bolting away like a cornered calf. Losing his balance in this melee, Adam falls to the floor, and I nearly follow him down. He lands on his side, and I slug him hard in the shoulder and stomp once on his upraised hip with my big-booted shoe. *A little of the old ultraviolence.* He's struggling to get away, as if he wants to literally worm his way through some legs toward the doorway. My chest is expanding, becoming lighter and more hollow; I'm thrilled and excited by this ugly display that I'm responsible for. Reeling with my own sense of power, my breathing is rapid and shallow.

"Fight! Fight! Fight!" the people behind me are chanting, like nasty kids in a school yard. To my surprise, Lisa, Adam's girlfriend, has kneeled down to pummel him with her tiny fists. Adam is now making occasional yelps.

"Why are you such an asshole!" she shouts, standing up to kick him in the back. "Why?" I join her in the stomping and pummeling.

"Say you're sorry, Adam," I tell him, pressing my shoe down on his outstretched arm. "Say it!"

"No!" He giggles, and I put more weight on his arm. *What if it breaks?* I'm surprised to discover that my answer to that is, *So it breaks. That'll teach him to sucker punch someone.* I ease off his arm to lean over and sock him hard, just below his ribs, a nice soft spot where my fist won't hit anything solid.

"Okay!" he hollers. "I'm sorry! I'm sorry!"

"Fine," I say, backing off. "Just don't do it again, or you'll really get it."

"Yeah!" says Lisa, straightening up. "Pick on someone your own size!"

Leaving them to each other, I brush past the onlookers to find Eli. He's in the kitchen, and as I finish my brief recap of Adam's reappearance, subsequent pounding, and Lisa's strange participation, Brad shows up to hand me my warm beer.

"So I hear Lynn beat the shit out of Adam," Eli says. I flush with pride.

"Dude," Brad says, solemnly shaking his head. "Not since the likes of Rodney King," he says, a little awed, "have I witnessed such a cruel beating."

"My protector," says Eli. And he's serious.

———

During a strength workout, I struggle to complete a chin-up; arms shaking, legs thrashing a little as my chin angles up, desperate to clear the bar. I'm not at Gleason's but at La Palestra, the gym on the Upper West Side, and I'm working out with Pat. A former semiprofessional hockey player and a former classics major at Brown, Pat has a pedantic tone, a teacher who questions and frustrates his students by forcing thought where rote motion would be a relief. His quiet confidence in my ability and his expectations in my performance remind me that he holds me to a higher physical standard than I do.

"Pull hard," commands Pat. "Kicking your legs isn't helping you." He's right, of course, and the foolishness of this gesture makes me laugh in spite of my heroic, eyeball-bursting effort. Pat's hand presses into the small of my back, giving me that vital nudge that enables me to finally complete the movement, gasping and panting.

"Now lower slowly," he says, "slowly," as I strain against gravity. My arms wobble and my descent is much quicker than I intended; I dangle briefly with my arms extended before hopping down to the gym floor. Groaning, I rub my upper arms. It was the last one of a set of three.

Men are better at chin-ups than women. They have a lower center of gravity and greater upper-body strength. When I left my husband and began training for the Marathon, I decided that chin-ups were my litmus test for manhood.

During that period, at the end of our twice-weekly circuit class, Pat made it a tradition for men and women to line up for the final exercise: chin-ups performed while the class cheered each person on. The women were expected to complete three, with varying degrees of assistance. A few could do one or two on their own, but some needed a nudge or push. Others required Pat to lift them up to the bar for all three. The men, on the other hand, had to execute six. Unassisted.

Most of the men in the class could crank out chin-up after chin-up, so Pat made them change their grip, or he occasionally hung on their legs. One evening there was a new guy in class, and when his turn came at the chinning bar, he could barely heave himself up for even one; his arms were shaking, and his face was set in a rictus of pain. My girlfriends and I exchanged shocked glances as we continued the polite cheering and clapping as Pat assisted his slow, agonizing ascent with both hands.

When we showered and dressed in the locker room, we discussed him in hushed tones. "Did you see that? He's not fat or anything."

"I've never seen a guy who couldn't do a chin-up!"

"I have, but this guy—"

"Yeah, he looked in better shape than a few others I could name"—pause for raucous laughter—"and they can all do six."

After dressing, five of us tracked Pat down and pulled him aside for an explanation. He looked at all of us as if we were total bitches.

"There's nothing *wrong* with him," he said, chuckling a little. "Not everyone can do a chin-up. He'll be able to do one soon, though." He raised an eyebrow that seemed to imply an unspoken end of the sentence: *unlike some of you.*

Soon after, Pat and I had a conversation about "my type of man." I chattered on about a sense of humor, good looks, intelligence, curiosity, a reader, someone who's fit, but not necessarily someone who works out in a gym.

"Would you go out with a guy who couldn't do as many push-ups and chin-ups as you could?"

"I would hope that I'm not so shallow as to—"

"Wrong!" he said.

"That's ridiculous. I don't want some goony football player, that's not my type at all!"

"I'm talking about a guy who can't do as many push-ups *as you.* You can do, at most, about twenty good ones in a row. How do you feel about a guy who can't do twenty push-ups?"

I stopped to consider this and shrugged my shoulders in exasperation. "So?" I pictured a faceless man struggling through a set of ten. "He can learn how to do more," I added with a self-conscious laugh, admitting defeat. "He can get better at it in no time."

Pat was satisfied that he'd proven his point, and I wondered: Do I really want a caveman to drag me back home by my hair? Is that what all of this fitness has come to?

When I admitted to my friends that I'd discovered an unexpected chink in my feminist armor—a real double standard—my male friends joked that I had a "physical fitness requirement" for potential boyfriends. Raphael, a screenwriter, has a whole comedy routine based on it: "Sure, you're a nice guy, you have a good job. But before she'll go out with you, she needs to know how fast you can run a mile. Seven minutes? Very good! And can you step over here to a chinning bar, sir? Oh, I'm sorry, you're going to have to do better than that. Why don't you work on that, come back in a few months, and you can retake the test again. Best of luck to you! *Next!*"

Eli was strong enough by those standards. But a year later, when he called me his protector, I knew we were close to the end.

THE PRELUDE

I'M STANDING IN the ring facing Sean, Hector's newest charge, a short, muscular Asian man in his late teens or early twenties. He's shirtless, in black trunks, and has a smudge of blood on his cheek from two brutal rounds with a very quick, wiry Hispanic boxer. Sean fights the way I used to, four months ago: no power, weak defensive skills, a pitiful offense, no real strategy except praying for the round to end quickly. In between rounds, Hector berated him for "hitting like a girl." His opponent, a former Olympian, has just hopped out of the ring with a look of disgust on his face; his perfectly white T-shirt carries a smear of Sean's blood.

Looking up, I meet Sean's eyes, then turn away. I'm supposed to be reciting my antifear mantra, which, I note with some dread, doesn't seem to have the same powerful effect it used to. It's possible it wears off, which would mean repeat business for the doctor, or maybe it's like a placebo, or religious faith; it works only if you believe it will. I think I can outbox Sean, but a terrified opponent is capable of anything; he outweighs me and has far more muscular strength. My right forearm throbs slightly under the tape Hector has used to buttress it. I landed a right punch wrong last week, which torqued my wrist as it skidded off target. My arm hasn't been the same since.

The bell rings. "We touch gloves," I say loudly, in case he's forgotten and wants to get off a sucker punch. Looking into his eyes when our gloves bump together, I try to reassure him with a steady gaze, then move around him lightly, easily, momentarily calming him down. He jabs me twice, and I can smell the adrenaline reek from his armpits. I let fly with a three-punch combination. Startled and scared, he bolts to all four corners. I can feel my big toe on my left foot throb in protest from the stops, starts, and fast turns.

"Protec' youself!" Hector yells at Sean. "Defense! Move aroun'! No' like that! With you body! Back and forth, in and out!" Sean is now crippled from fear of Hector's raging verbal abuse and the horror of being beaten by a woman. He aims for my face, the target of choice for the novice,

241

bent on a knockout blow, anything to cut short the round. Chasing him, I catch his temple a couple of times, his ribs once.

When the bell rings, I walk to Hector, and Sean is waved over by Gilbert. Spitting out my mouthpiece, I listen to Hector's tirade. "Why you not fighting! You stan' there, you fight! Bam, bam, thees way, that way! Don' just move aroun'! Use the jab!" Swallowing, I open my mouth. He pours in the precious liquid, a cooling balm against my gums, hot and raw from the friction of the mouthguard. "Use combinations! Use the jab, keep heem away! Jab, jab, jab!"

We go through two more rounds, and it's only in the last one that I remember Sean had a bloody nose when we started. A nose that's already started to bleed will bleed again very easily. Concentrating on nothing but head shots, I catch him several times before striking vermilion: both nostrils start to ooze. Hitting him with a right, my glove skids off his slick upper lip, and a stab of pain shoots down my forearm.

The bell rings, and as I walk over to Hector, I see a tall, brown-haired girl in street clothes watching me from across the gym. I recognize her as the snotty girl who trains with Angel. I think her name's Carol.

"She fight you," says Hector, taking off my headgear.

"Hey," Sean says, before I can fully absorb this news. He touches my shoulder with his glove as he exits the ring: "You had some good punches."

242

"Thanks. Good job," I tell him, before turning back to Hector. This woman is my opponent this Saturday. "So she saw me fight just now?"

"She don' spar," Hector says, untying my gloves, still king of the non sequitur. "Speed bag. Three round."

For the next several minutes, I have one eye on my work-out, one eye on hers. Carol works with Angel on the mitts. He's talking, but she doesn't say a word and never cracks a smile. Her movements are slow and methodical and not, to my eye, particularly powerful.

"You fight her?" A boxer at a speed bag next to mine shakes me out of my reverie during the round break.

"Me? Not yet. Saturday."

"She hits hard," he says.

"Yeah?" A ball of fire erupts from the pit of my stomach as I resist the urge to press for details. Maybe he's a friend of hers.

"I sparred with her once," he says. "She hit hard."

————

On Wednesday Carol and I arrive at the gym at the same time and wordlessly change together in the locker room. I'm trying to convey the impression that she doesn't concern me one way or the other. I try not to focus on the fact that she has four years of experience, a three-inch height advantage, and eight extra pounds on me.

This day she does spar. She's in the ring closest to the ladies' room, the one farthest from Hector's usual choice for his boxers. It's as if she's trying to be as discreet about it as possible. She's boxing a man who's not wearing any headgear, a shirtless black guy who weaves slowly around her: Angel, her trainer. She takes one step forward and throws a punch. One step to the side, throws another. Step, punch, step, punch. Can't she move and hit at the same time?

Hector sees me watching her. "She no good. She no spar."

On my way home from the gym, I stop in at my doctor's office. He told me this morning he would be able to squeeze me in today.

"I think I have some sort of food poisoning," I tell him, my legs dangling off the end of the examination table. The protective paper I'm sitting on was freshly dispensed from a large roll by a nurse who took my blood pressure. It squeaks against the leather as I talk and shift my hands around. Dr. Goldberg is sitting on a rolling wooden chair and scoots away from me a little so he can put his legs up on a filing cabinet. He looks at me, waiting for details.

"Every morning this week, I've had an upset stomach. I woke up on Monday and didn't feel right. Cramps, upset stomach. Felt better that afternoon. But every morning I feel awful. It's just not going away. Last time I had this— what, four years ago?—I thought it was appendicitis. Turned out to be a parasite. I was on strong antibiotics and had to eat just rice for days."

"When's your fight?" He laces his hands behind his head and is staring up at the ceiling.

"Yes!" I say, excited that he's already taken this into consideration. "Exactly! It's Saturday, so I don't know if it's such a great idea to take massive antibiotics. Then again, feeling ill isn't much of a strategy either. What do you think?"

"What do I think?" he says, putting his feet down and scooting closer. "Have you ever heard the term *scared shitless*?" There's a pause in our conversation, and I can hear another patient in the next room laughing with the nurse. My mouth is slightly agape, wondering where this is leading.

"Yes, I've heard the term," I finally say.

"You don't have food poisoning."

"But the symptoms are exactly—"

"There's something called the fight-or-flight syndrome. Do you know what an animal does when it's scared, right before it has to run?" His eyebrows are raised, but he's lost me. "It shits. It's a natural reflex." He folds his arms.

"You're saying this is . . . nerves," I say, dragging the word out. He nods.

"That doesn't mean you can't treat it," he says. "It's just not food poisoning. Take one tablet of Imodium in the morning. Over-the-counter medicine. That should take care of things." He stands up and claps me on the shoulder, an effort at cheering me up.

"You're sure about this," I say, feeling foolish, but acknowledging his diagnosis has the ring of truth.

Whenever I think about next Saturday night at Gleason's,

I become suddenly claustrophobic, my heart rate zooms into overdrive, sweat springs from my armpits, and my skin feels like slick, mildewed vinyl.

Odd, but in the days leading up to the fight, I don't panic in the ring. I panic everywhere else. Dr. Halpin's hypnosis has not removed fear, it's just diverted it from the particular arena of boxing. Like a river that has changed course, it's now spilling into other, previously anxiety-free areas. I'm wheeling a grocery cart down the aisle in the supermarket, and I'm inexplicably afraid of a large tower of paper towels. I smell cologne on my doorman and start to tremble. While pulling on my socks in the locker room, I'm short of breath, but put me in the ring, and like magic, I can think clearly again.

On Friday, it's my turn with the Avenging Olympian, the one who fought Sean. A large crowd has gathered at the bench opposite the ring and near the door. Hector is laughing and joking with a few guys in Spanish. He's pointing at me and raising his fists, shaking his head admiringly. The Avenger smiles, a cruel grin, like he's going to relish scooping out my eyeballs and eating them off a skewer. I see his gold tooth, a shiny yellow incisor. I smile back, as pleasantly as possible. *You don't scare me.* After all, it's impossible: I'm in a boxing ring. Gilbert leans in with his mouthpiece, and the Avenger leans over to gobble it from his outstretched palm like a horse eating a carrot.

The bell rings, and he's on me as if I were magnetized.

We couldn't be closer if we were dancing; he's drinking in all of my oxygen. There's a clattering and a thumping from his fists that sound like someone running up a staircase, except they're landing on my body. The entire effect, if it weren't so brutal, would be nearly comical. I'm half-smiling with the absurdity of it as I fold up into a crouch. He eases up, and I rise slightly. "Hey!" I gasp out, gripping him around his arms, instigating a clinch. "Hey!" I tell him softly. "Slow down, man!" We break apart, and I hop backward, arms up, feeling as if I've been shaken all over.

He stands still and smiles again, revealing an odd-looking mouthpiece. It's been customized: white with a sliver of gold, just like his dental work. I clear my head with a little shake—then with all of my strength, I deliver the hardest jab I can. My body leans forward with the momentum, and his head rocks back, but that's all the satisfaction I get; next thing I know there's a tremendous pain in my left side. Not those ribs again, dear Lord. Please, no broken ribs. "Motherfucker," I growl at him. So much for being able to see everything faster—I don't even know which hand delivered that punch. I catch him in the side of his face with a right; he nearly ducks it, but I get lucky. We grapple in a clinch again, and my face is crushed into his neck; at least he won't be able to hit it. The bell rings.

I stomp over to Hector, who's smiling crazily. I frown momentarily, confused. Where's the tirade? Are the spectators inhibiting him for some reason?

"Ha! You doin' good!" He delicately removes my mouthpiece with two fingers and holds up the water bottle with upraised eyebrows. As I take in water, he nods at me, as if to say, "He's an animal, right?" Two spectators, Hispanic men in their thirties, in sport jackets and open-collared shirts, give me a thumbs-up. I raise a glove, still swallowing. One claps politely, applause appropriate to a golf tournament. Gilbert shakes hands with one of them and sits down to watch.

The second round is even worse. I gasp after he catches me in the forehead. Throwing two jabs, I barely notice an uppercut on its way to my sternum. "Ooooof!" Laying the reaction on thick, I expect him to back off. Instead, he's excited by it and practically climbs on top of me in an effort to wedge his fist between my arms, digging in toward my face.

Shaking him loose, I pull back, then charge forward and catch him in the lip, right at the gold tooth. I throw a wild swing that sails by his head, but the next, an uppercut, connects with his forearm. The bell finally rings, and I stagger, breathless, over to Hector, who's laughing proudly.

"I'm fighting tomorrow, Hector, and I'm getting real tired."

"Oh! Shit!" Hector blanches. "Ho-kay! Out!" I smile cheerfully at the Avenger, raising a glove. A smattering of applause breaks out as I step down. Gilbert stands and walks over to us.

"Maybe they want to sponsor you," says Gilbert. "You know, when you turn pro next week."

"Yeah, sure," I say, taking a speed bag from Hector, and then I see Carol standing across the room.

When Hector laces me back into my gloves for the heavy bag, she's already working out there herself. The only free space is directly next to her, and so we pound away at the big swinging bags like gravediggers, working side by side. Hector is quiet but is watching protectively. When the round bell sounds, he walks over with a dampened towel and wipes down my face, offers me a drink.

Hector waves me back over toward the door to work with the mitts. It occurs to me that I have exactly six minutes to perfect my right uppercut. A quick combination of arm and wrist, rising up and turning. We go over and over the motion. "Hard!" he says, bracing himself with the mitt held high. "Hard!" He raises it slightly. Right: her chin will be right about there. Exhaling, I concentrate: arm, wrist, power, turn.

"Sí!" Hector says, satisfied. The bell rings. My wrist is killing me. Hector pulls off my gloves, my wraps, the tape. "You go home, eat, get some sleep," he says, fussing with rewinding the wraps just so. "No boyfrien'."

"No," I tell him, smiling a little at the widely held belief that sex before a fight means reduced aggression, weakened legs. "No boyfriend."

"You get sleep, eat a nice breakfast, relax all day, come back tomorrow."

"See you then." I want to tell him how much I appreciate the way he didn't yell or berate me in front of Carol, the spectators, the Avenger, but I don't know how to explain it so he'll understand. "Thanks, Hector."

He nods briefly and hands me my gear.

THE FIGHT

THANKSGIVING IS JUST over two weeks away when nine of us board the train out to Brooklyn. My world has become so small, so fixated on this one day, that I haven't made any plans beyond it. Eli has my video camcorder, and Anne, one of my best friends, and Mark, the photographer who accompanied me to the Golden Gloves, have cameras. Kristin and Raphael, married screenwriters and close neighbors of mine, are here with their friend Eric. Both he and Mark have brought dates, women I've just met for the first time.

My other friends, my workout buddies, are running the New York Marathon tomorrow and consequently couldn't join this little group. They're staying over at a friend's house conveniently located just blocks away from the starting line in Staten Island, and they're probably eating a big meal of pasta at this very moment. I promised to call later and tell them how it went, and to wish them a final good luck. My hand in my coat pocket is toying with the slip of paper that has their phone number scribbled on it, and the two quarters for the pay phone are warm from my touch. When I take these out and use them, the fight will be over.

We pass the time on the train by joking around and talking about everything except where they're going: to watch me fight.

Mine is only one of several fights scheduled at Gleason's tonight. The rest of the program lists bouts primarily between men who've traveled here from boxing clubs and gyms in the Bronx and Staten Island. Gleason's boxers, though not necessarily better, have the home court advantage. There are about 150 people there; the majority of them are local supporters: either they train at Gleason's or are friends with people who do. Despite the crowd out front, the locker room is empty when I go in with two of my girlfriends.

I take special care in dressing, methodically proceeding step by step, worried about forgetting some crucial element that I'll realize only when I'm in the ring, when it's too late. Pulling on my favorite black unitard, I sit down to rub

Vaseline on my feet and to patch the blood blister on my left toe with a piece of moleskin. Using the tiny pair of scissors I keep in my locker for just this task, I carefully nip at its edges so it lies just right.

"Boy, you're prepared," says Kristin.

"Nervous?" says Anne, a magazine editor. I nod in response, too superstitious to say the word, and also because I'm concentrating hard on swallowing. My mouth is filling up with spit, and I can't seem to breathe and swallow simultaneously.

There's a brand-new, fluffy set of Thorlo padded sports socks in my bag, purchased especially for the occasion. "Life is always better with fresh socks," I tell my friends in a weak attempt at humor. Slowly tucking my cosseted feet into my wrestling sneakers, I stand up and stamp them a few times, checking for any bunching.

"Left foot feels funny," I murmur, pulling the shoe off, straightening the sock seam at the toes, and then carefully sliding it back in. Satisfied, I lace the sneakers up and tuck the shoelace ends neatly behind the tongue. Moving over to the mirror, I braid my hair and fasten two barrettes to the side of my head to hold back some shorter wisps. Checking my profile, I reposition one farther back; a few months ago I learned the hard way that getting hit on a flat metal barrette, even through the headgear, can mean a nasty little scalp cut.

My preparations complete, I ask if they want to stow their coats or purses in my locker. They hesitate a moment and then wedge everything in. The door is slammed, and the lock is squeezed closed.

Bruce has a table set up outside of his office where boxers are to check in and pay the twenty-five-dollar entry fee, an amount to cover the expense of the chrome trophies—a boxer perched atop a tall pedestal, throwing a jab—to be awarded to everyone who participates. I'm disappointed to learn that no winners will be announced. Still, the crowd will choose its favorite and that will have to be enough. The current lineup is posted on a list Scotch-taped down next to the strongbox; there are seven fights, and mine is the fifth. All boxers are required to weigh in on the scale next to Bruce and to sign a waiver, the details of which I barely scan. A litany of injuries and unexpected death scenarios is not something I need to worry about before I strap on my headgear.

"Heeyyyy!" a familiar voice calls out. It's Dominick. He looks cleaner than usual, nicely shaved, his hair shiny and brushed, dressed neatly in a white T-shirt, blue jeans, and sneakers.

"Hey," I answer back.

"I'm the ref tonight!" he says, arms outstretched. My face freezes. A joke, right? Glancing at Bruce, he nods.

"Great. I'm sure you'll judge fairly."

"Good luck to you," he says, smiling his shark smile. My stomach rolls.

Taking the time to swallow the mass of saliva that's

again materialized in my mouth, I turn to Kristin and say, "That's the guy. Who beat me up. He's the ref."

"Oh, honey," she says, giving me a hug. I burst out laughing, a combination of hysteria and panic that my opponent, her trainer, or her friends might be looking on and would see this embrace as a needed comfort for my anxiety.

Fight number three is between two women from the same gym in Staten Island. As they start, it's clear that neither one has been boxing very long, and it would appear to be the first time either has sparred. Punches are thrown with eyes squeezed shut and heads ducked down or turned away. Neither one defends herself, so they take turns absorbing blows, a Punch and Judy–style puppet show. Bruce is the timekeeper, and after witnessing one round of terrible boxing, starts round two, only to end it ten seconds later, after seeing an even sharper decline in their abilities.

"That was a bit quick, wasn't it?" says Mark. The crowd seems torn between laughter and protestation. The ref glances at Bruce, who briefly nods his head.

"Let's hear a round of applause for the ladies," says Dominick, with uncharacteristic kindness. The crowd dutifully responds. The girls squeal with delight as they're each presented with identical trophies.

Carol is talking to her trainer near the locker room. She's wearing a Gleason's T-shirt, a brilliant strategic touch; some people might assume I'm the outsider here. A red scarf ties back her hair under her headgear, which matches her red gloves. Hector catches my eye and waves me over, holding up the roll of tape for my wrist. I squeeze out from my row and walk with him over to a bench near his office, behind the crowd, so he can get to work. As usual, Hector displays an incredible gift for intuiting exactly how much pressure should be applied. My wraps go on next, then my gloves and headgear. He carries a small white towel, my mouthguard, and a bottle of water over to our corner of the ring, and we wait for the fight in progress to end.

David, the Renegade Jew, has just bloodied the nose of his opponent. Blood splashes the canvas. *What the hell am I doing here?* They move out, we step in. I am calm, I am sharp, I am elusive, I am vicious.

Carol and I are introduced by Bruce to loud cheers as "the big event of the evening." To my surprise, it sounds as if he means it. We're beckoned into the center of the ring by Dominick, who sternly summarizes the rules of boxing. I'm far too preoccupied by the stunning and unfamiliar presence of a crowd to listen to him: their noises and rumblings, the smell of 150 people exhaling in a place where I'm going to need to suck in as much air as possible, the odd and distracting scraps of conversation. "Yo, Tina!" a man calls out, and it's all I can do to resist the urge to help him scan the crowd for her. The assemblage takes up a surprisingly large chunk of mental space, with its pressure to perform, my fear of failure in their eyes, the self-consciousness of being on display in a skintight leotard.

Who can concentrate on boxing, with all this going on? My friends are smiling.

Carol and I touch gloves, hop backward to our corners, and Bruce sounds the bell. Our first jabs meet headlong before we both exchange a flurry of blows; I resort to a barrage of jabs to keep her away, to wait until the hysteria of the opening seconds subsides. She throws two punches simultaneously, both arms flying up—a silly blunder due to nerves. *I'm sure she didn't mean to do that,* I think in a momentary flash of empathy, but I nevertheless duck down to catch her in her unprotected ribs, then tap her on the side of her head. Her eyes roll wildly away from my fist like those of a spooked horse. It's a moment that starts to hang up, taking longer to complete than usual.

Until this evening, I thought boxers were so focused in the ring that the crowd receded from their consciousness. I imagined they experienced the crowd in much the same way as a rock star: just one big blur of noise. But tonight I can hear everyone and everything they say. I'm in the center of a giant game of charades, where every move provokes another opinion.

"Take her! Knock her down!"

"Move in, all right!"

"Pop it!"

Carol's fist blocks most of my jabs halfway, but one slips past and lands on her nose. Her eyes glitter crazily.

"Jab, Leen!" Hector's voice rises above the din. "Tha's it! Good!"

She hits my face hard, twice, and nausea, like seasickness, washes over me. Still, we continue our slow clockwise tango to the left. Recovering my equilibrium, I successfully evade several of her jabs by ducking my head. Then I lash out at her ribs. The round ends just after she smashes a right into my cheekbone.

"You doin' very good out there, *very* good," Hector says gently, squirting water into my open mouth. His encouragement is such a relief, I nearly start crying. "Make sure you arm comes back fast!" He demonstrates, quickly pulling his fist close to his chest. It dawns on me that my arms must be hanging out there in the air after each punch, which is why she's able to hit me in the head. "You look good, doin' good." He rinses my mouthpiece and puts it back in. "You okay, doin' great." Biting down, I turn to face her and to wait for the bell. Angel is still talking to her, making big animated gestures, as if he's narrating a children's story. The round bell sounds.

Carol runs at me with a fury that literally stops me in my tracks. Four punches land on me within the space of two seconds, three to my head, the last one snapping my head to the side and up; the sight of the ceiling is terrifying. Am I going down? Barely recovering, I dart to the right.

Coming back hard to her ribs, I throw a right to her jaw, but it's deflected by her glove. Another right to her face, and her lips pull back to reveal a white mouthpiece, clear back to its edges. I hear Hector's chant of "Jab! Jab! Jab! Jab!" The audience is roaring louder now, the surges in their enthusiasm corresponding exactly to the landing of each punch, an obvious fact that suddenly appalls me. *This is like getting into a car accident for sport* is what goes through my mind, the sudden absurdity of boxing and my place in it.

Carol smashes me hard in the nose, the tip folding down on itself in a way I wouldn't have believed possible, mashing into my upper lip. The force of her fist grinds my mouthguard into every possible surface of my gums, tearing and ripping the soft tissue as if it were a razor. A numbing, tingling sensation spreads from my nose along the sides of my face, and heat pours into my sinuses, spreading backward into my throat. My upper torso rockets to the side with the momentum, and somehow my legs catch up and move under me. I'm spared any further punishment for the moment, but only because she's as exhausted as I am.

Both of us throw jabs as we follow each other in a clockwise circle around the ring. She's staring at me as if I'm planning to kill her whole family and burn down her home; as if her one chance at survival is to find the kitchen knife and plunge it deep into my heart. Her face is contorting, her eyes wide, mouth shifting from snarling to pleading to determination. I've never fought anyone who looked at me this way; maybe this is how I'm looking at her, how I've looked at all my sparring partners.

I land a right to her face, and the force of it expels spit and mucus from her mouth and nose. A fine spray now rests on the part of her headgear just near her cheek.

My eyes move to her nostrils, waiting for the appearance of blood. We're poised like this for what seems like minutes, hours. Suddenly I wonder if I'll be standing in this ring until time rolls to a complete stop. How sad never again to swim in the ocean, never to lie down in sweet-smelling grass, or see my family again. I have no idea how much real time is passing; within this little bit of eternity, Carol hits me twice, and I jab back weakly. Eli is chanting "Strong! Strong!" when the bell finally rings.

Hector offers water, soothing advice. My gums are raw from the mouthpiece, I swish the cool liquid around as a balm. He reassures me that my nose isn't bleeding, my big concern at this moment. "You doin' good!" he says. "You doin' jus' fine. She running! She scared of you!"

"Really?"

"Yes!" Hector rinses the mouthguard and gently slides it in. I bite down, wincing. No matter what, it's just two more minutes: I don't have to pace myself, I can give it my all. After that, it's over.

The bell sounds, and again Carol flies out of her corner, her head reared back, her expression somewhere between hysteria and determination as she throws four desperate blows. Both of her hands swing wildly around my head and neck, so I tuck my chin to my chest and pound at her ribs. She leaps back, then runs forward, grabbing me in a clinch. "Don' stop, baby!" Hector yells. "Don' stop!" I plant a left into her ribs, and she eases back enough for me to swing at her face. We revolve again, both throwing jabs, batting them away. I can see she's wiped out, but I only wish I had the strength to capitalize on it.

Angel's voice soars over the crowd. "Pop it!" he says. "Pop it!" She throws a left hook that lands neatly, by the book, right on my left temple. Staggering to the side, I recover to throw a few more jabs and land a right to her head as the bell rings. Dominick flings himself between us, but we drop our arms and push him aside so we can quickly embrace. I don't feel warmth from her, and I'm sure she doesn't feel it from me. We're standing still for a time, just resting before we have to make the long walk to our corners. The fight is over.

Hector is leaping up and down, arms raised triumphantly, smiling, bursting with pride. He gives me a big hug and rushes around to hug Carol. Dominick walks over and claps me on the shoulder. "You did it!" he says. There's an incredible uproar. The crowd is yelling and I think it's for me. I get another hug from Hector, and a kiss on the neck. He removes my headgear as Bruce enters the ring again.

"Presenting the trophies for this bout," he says, "is the contender for the world title, Merqui Sosa." A tall light heavyweight in a nylon jacket with matching pants doffs his baseball cap as an acknowledgment of the applause. He hands Carol and me identical trophies, and the three of us pose for a photo.

Climbing down out of the ring, I see my friends coming over to me. Another fight is just starting, so the crowd's attention has moved on to new business. "I never thought I'd see you again," I say to Eli. He's pointing the video camera at me.

"What?" he says, peering at me through the viewfinder. "I was screaming for you!"

Anne and Mark are busy snapping photos of me clutching my trophy. Cameras are passed around, clusters of friends form and re-form around me.

"You were awesome," says Kristin. "Awesome!" I'm smiling like crazy, but it's because I'm finally out of purgatory. Eli ushers me over to Hector, who removes my gloves and wraps.

"She scared of you! Four year she boxes! You beat her!"

Another boxer darts over and bumps his fist into my glove. "Good fight, man! You killed her!"

I nod and smile, grateful it's all over. "She didn't touch me here," I say, running my hands down my sides. Hector hands me my gear, and I quickly walk into the locker room, pausing for a moment before opening the door. Is she in here? No; it's empty. Opening my locker, I grab the roll of paper towels and liquid soap and head for the sink.

Tipping my head back, I see a triangle of red under my nose. Dabbing with a wet paper towel, there's a tiny smear of blood from one nostril. Lifting up my lip, there's purple bruising, and tiny cuts along my gumline. My eyes are a little puffy, as if I've been crying. Splashing cold water on my face, I wash up quickly and carefully blot dry. Hurrying back over to my locker, I unlace my sneakers, rip down my unitard, and yank off my socks.

Pulling Anne and Kristin's coats and purses out of my locker, I throw my headgear and gloves back in, slam it shut, and stagger out. The effort of carrying everything makes my face, particularly my nose, throb in protest. Is it possible to get a nosebleed this way? Practically tossing them their belongings, I fish a quarter out of my pocket, and that scrap of paper.

"Bruce," I hiss at him, as he gathers up his papers from the table next to the ring, "did I win?"

He looks down at a piece of paper and takes a moment before saying softly, "I have you taking rounds one and three, with Carol taking round two."

"So I won."

He shrugs. I take that as a yes.

PANIC

THE MORNING AFTER the fight, I'm supposed to spend most of the day on the corner of First Avenue and Sixty-eighth Street, to cheer on my friends as they pass by in the Marathon. At the end of the race, there's going to be a party at my gym for the Marathoners, as it's perfectly located half a block from the finish line. I'm one of the two dozen members who've volunteered to wait at checkpoints along the route with bananas, orange slices, Gatorade, and water bottles. But right now I'm scared to leave my bathroom. I can't shake the feeling that someone's out there, waiting to beat me up.

My paranoia began the night before. For weeks I'd been looking forward to my postfight victory celebration at the opening of a friend's new restaurant, and so I shook my head adamantly when Eli suggested that it might be better to stay in. "I want to eat a steak, I want some wine, I want to relax," I said peevishly. "I'll just hop in the shower, get dressed, put some ice on my face for a little while, take some Advil, and we can go. I'll be ready in twenty minutes."

The restaurant, located on a small side street in SoHo, was a madhouse by the time we arrived at eleven. People were crowding the bar and spilling into the eating area, surrounding the seated guests. Holding my hand, Eli hauled me through the mob.

A blonde with bright red lipstick muscled her way toward us, shoving me aside with enough force to knock me off my balance. Pulling Eli's hand to try and right myself, I fell into a man in a leather jacket standing at the bar, stepping indelicately on his foot. "I'm so sorry," I told him, grateful that my aching nose didn't smash into his chest.

Eli and I pushed on again. Suddenly, there wasn't nearly enough air in the room. All the smoke, all these people. A small wave of panic began to rise, but it subsided once I saw a woman holding menus. "Miss!" I yelled over the din. "Is it possible to get a table for two, please?"

She waved at us to follow her, and we clawed our way deeper into the restaurant, to a smaller, much less crowded back room. She cheerfully gestured at a small table in a corner and put down two menus.

"Thanks! So much!" I said, plopping into a chair, absurdly thrilled at this magically free table. Eli sat down. "Does my face look okay?" I said. "You know, normal?"

"Uhhhmmmm . . ." he said, squinting, his head tilted.

"Never mind. I just got my answer." I turned my attention to the menu, gingerly touching the bridge of my nose. That was when I sensed it coming: something big hurtling toward me. My right forearm flew up to protect my face, and I ducked. My left hand curled tightly around the laminated menu, and my legs tensed under the table, one lashing out and kicking Eli.

"Can I tell you about our specials?" The big, scary thing rushing toward my skull was our waiter solicitously bending over the table to tell us about the food.

"You okay over there?" said Eli. I nodded slowly, trying to look calm. When the waiter's lips stopped moving, I smiled and asked for a glass of red wine.

"I keep seeing her," I told Eli when our waiter left.

"Seeing who?"

Seeing who. "My opponent," I said, enunciating. "I see that look in her eyes. She wanted to kill me before I killed her."

"You're just having a delayed reaction," he said. "Are you getting an appetizer?"

———

I woke up the next morning, on the day of the Marathon, with a start, as if from a nightmare. Eli didn't stay

over, having mentioned something about attending a fu-
neral early today, although he was vague about whose. I actually was relieved to say good-bye after our late dinner
last night, impatient to go home, to bolt and chain the door,
to pack ice around my face, and to finally be alone. But
now in the morning, shaking in my bed, near tears, unsure
of what scared me and why, I wish he were here, even
though the relationship is unraveling. I wish my mother
were here too, if she would promise not to tell me I brought
all of this on myself. I wish anyone were here.

While inspecting my ruined face in the bathroom mirror,
I turn on the all-news radio station. The forecast is for bit-
terly cold temperatures, which is bad news for the runners
but good news for me, as my face will feel iced anytime
I'm outdoors. Bundled up and ready to leave, I try on my
sunglasses to see if they cover any of the more dramatic
bruises, but they don't, and the weight of them is painful
on my nose, so I wrap a scarf around the bottom of my face
and set off for the subway. Half a block later, I pull it down:
the chafing of the material is unbearable against my raw,
sensitive skin.

On the uptown train, I realize that two women and a man
on the opposite side of the car are regarding me with some
concern. Quickly dropping my gaze, I pretend to root
around inside my purse for something, trying to keep the
underside of my nose out of view. A woman with a banged-
up face is always a victim. A man could still come off as a

tough guy. Should I tell them I'm a boxer? The train stops, and they get off: a moot point.

Happy to think about anything other than boxing or last night, a couple hours of standing in the cold makes everyone's face look purpled and bruised; my injuries are eventually forgotten and pass unremarked upon. As I watched my friends run past, it seems incredible that I was in their shoes only a year ago. This time last year, I thought boxing sounded interesting, that it would put me in the best shape of my life, that I was tired of taking crap from guys, and that I wanted to know the pure pleasure of violence. This time last year, running in this race, I'd never been beaten up.

Back in the gym, when the party is in full swing, people are asking about the fight, my injuries, if I want to sit down. The Broadway actress Betty Buckley walks over at one point to ask me, gently, "Should you be doing this to your face?"

I shrug off her concern, chugging more wine. "Hey, I could fall down in the shower and get hurt much worse," I tell her, reflexively giving the standard response usually reserved for my parents. "I'm a writer," I tell her. "We don't have to be attractive."

"Don't be so eager to get rid of your looks," she tells me. "They'll go away soon enough."

———

Four days pass before I can bring myself to watch the videotape of the fight. The first time I see it, I'm alone, curled up on the couch, my stomach in a knot, every muscle poised and tense. My hand rests on the remote, ready to turn it off if it gets too much. The images flicker on my television, and even though I know exactly what happens, I'm terrified. Flinching with every blow thrown, I will my video image to throw more jabs, to protect my face.

After the fight ends, the tape jumps to a shot of me sitting on this same couch, a bag of ice at my face. It takes me a moment to figure out that this occurred before we went out to dinner. I have absolutely no memory of it happening. Eli asks me questions about the fight, and as I watch the tape, I'm surprised to hear my answers. In between questions, I look over at Eli behind the camera and regard him warily.

I tell my friend Anne that I don't even like to think about the fight, much less talk about it.

"You probably have post-traumatic stress syndrome," she says.

"No, it's just an unpleasant experience that I don't particularly want to relive." But it's not just the fight: anything that recalls boxing gives me the shakes. The bell that announces the closing of subway doors, a poster for an upcoming bout on Pay-Per-View, even a black leather club chair in a furniture showroom makes me walk away, disturbed by how much it recalls headgear and gloves. Am I still so angry, and so terrified of being thought of as cowardly that I have to box for the rest of my life? I have my proof, I went the distance, and now it's time to stop.

The sensation I carry everywhere is the shock of waking up from a horrible nightmare: I dreamed I was a boxer for a year. The crap was beaten out of me three times a week, my trainer was a bully. Then I had a big fight where a whole crowd of people screamed for my blood and my opponent's blood. Then I woke up.

In the four years that have passed since I've boxed, I've moved from enthusiastic and knowledgeable fight fan to queasy, reluctant spectator. It would be simplistic to say that the reason I don't enjoy watching people box anymore is because it makes me relive my own experiences, but it's more than that. It reminds me of how close I came to damaging myself permanently, all to prove how fearless I was, to settle a score that was started back in the sixth grade when I was pushed off the swings by a bully, and that sensation of helplessness was dramatically revived during my divorce. I wanted to feel powerful, to take up space in the world, to stop apologizing. That I thought I could do this by learning how to fight now strikes me as ludicrous and deranged. I don't even have the luxury of wondering why no one tried to talk me out of such a stupid idea. "There was just no talking to you," says my brother, an apt assessment of my determination.

I start realizing all of this during the week immediately

following my fight, when my friends ask me over and over: "When's your next bout?"

There would be no next bout. I'd had it.

———

Ten days later, when my face looks normal again, I take my last subway ride to Gleason's to clean out my locker. Walking down the hill, I'm cheered by the thought that I won't ever have to see this sidewalk, wait for this light; this entire experience, this huge part of my life, is now over: the panic attacks, the bloody noses, the injured ribs, the bruised eyes, the swollen hands, the damaged feet. Over. Coming up the stairs, the metallic, musky tang of Gleason's wafts over me, and I can't help it, my heart pounds in my chest: *You're in danger, you're in danger.*

Hector, Gigo, Raymond, Arturo, and guys whose names I don't even know cheer when they see me, high fives all around, gloves tapped or shaken.

"You fight me today," says Ray, who meets me first.

"Nah, I'm just here to get my stuff," I tell him. His eyes widen and he starts to speak, but I walk toward the locker room. Once I have my gear with me, it'll be easier to make my getaway.

The locker room, as usual, is empty, and for that I'm relieved. Opening my lock, I remove it from the door and place it in my gym bag. My headgear, gloves, a notebook, a box of Band-Aids; the detritus of the past year gets quickly shoved in. The bag is zipped. Slamming the locker shut, I consider the masking-tape label on the door bearing my name. After carefully peeling it off, I almost throw it in the trash, but I can't stand the thought of leaving part of me here. I stuff it into my purse instead and head back out to the big room.

My comment to Ray and all that it implied spread quickly while I was packing up. Hector looks shocked, crestfallen. Arturo stands nearby and stares at me, unsmiling, bewildered. Ray holds up a glove, a final salute.

Gigo steps forward, blocking my path to Hector. "We have an investment in you," he says seriously. "Now you're good, we train you, you can't just quit, leave us." The threat hangs in the air.

How can I explain to him the complicated algebra of bravado and fear? How can I explain that there are some things in life worth being scared of? I look at these men and I respect their values and their codes of honor, but I also know that I can't be part of their world anymore. The physical and emotional cost is far too great. And most important of all, it's time to get back to having a real life.

"I'm moving to California," I say, lying through my teeth.

"California!" Hector says, smiling again, perhaps with relief: my leaving him isn't personal. "Hollywood?"

"Yeah, Hollywood," I say. "I'm moving. I'll have to find a gym out there." I manage a smile. "Thanks, Hector," I say, handing over an eight-by-ten color photo of us on the night of the fight, posing with my trophy.

"You quit?" he says, shaking the hand I've proffered, turning it into a hug.

"No, no, just leaving," I say.

"Moving with you boyfriend?"

"Yes, that's what I'm doing."

"Good," he says, satisfied. I'm released from his grasp.

"I'll come back and visit sometime," I say, knowing I won't. Walking out quickly now, I smile and wave at Gigo, Arturo, and Ray. Gloves are raised, and Gigo glowers: he knows I am lying.

AFTERWORD

IF I HAD known then what I know now, I would have never gotten into a ring.

Reggie Tuur said he wanted to get out of boxing with his faculties still intact. A nine-year veteran, his plan was early retirement, "in a few years." He may very well stay sharp into old age, but he's betting his brains on old research. Until recently, a short career was thought to be the best way to avoid ending up as a dazed, shuffling, palsied former boxer, to escape whatever it was that happened to Muhammad Ali.

Ali had, later on in his career, nearly abandoned the brilliant evasive actions that coincided with his "float like a butterfly, sting like a bee" motto, preferring the crowd-pleasing drama of "rope-a-dope." This scenario required Ali to allow himself to be beaten mercilessly, offering little resistance, and then when all hope seemed lost, he would rise up and stage a dramatic comeback in the later rounds, emerging as the victor. This strategy provided wonderful suspense for spectators, but his discovery that he could take a punch, rather than neatly avoid one, may have been his Faustian bargain.

With this sort of damning evidence offered by ex-boxers, it was previously believed that debilitating brain damage by the age of forty or fifty was caused not by one blow but by a long career of head injuries. The most vulnerable candidates are the boxers renowned, and even celebrated, for their ability to "take a punch." Muhammad Ali and his family and handlers contend that his Parkinson's disease has nothing to do with his time in the ring, even though boxers are afflicted with it (and with multiple sclerosis and Alzheimer's) in far greater numbers than the general population.

Another boxer, Jerry Quarry, was also a heavyweight contender in the late 1960s and early 1970s and is most often touted as the textbook example of "punch drunk syndrome," or *dementia pugilistica*. Quarry first put on boxing gloves at the age of three and won a junior Golden Gloves title at eight. In his twenties, as another "Great White

Hope," he fought, and was brutally beaten by, Ali, Joe Frazier, and Floyd Patterson, in fights that were stopped not because Quarry went down but because it was determined that he could take no more punishment, however eager he was for the opportunity. Quarry was often described as having "heart," that willingness to endure pain in order to inflict it.

By the age of fifty, however, he was suffering from severe memory loss, resting tremors, crippled motor skills, and third-stage dementia. His millions of dollars in earnings long gone, Jerry relied on Social Security disability checks and his brother for full-time care. This around-the-clock attention was needed for even the simplest of tasks, as the ex-boxer could no longer tie his own shoes, shower, shave, cut his food, or feed himself. Interviewed for a television news program in 1996, Jerry looked confused and dazed; when asked to sign a pair of boxing gloves at the Boxing Hall of Fame, Jerry looked at his brother and in a low, halting voice asked, "How do you make a Q?" At the age of fifty-three, unable to recall or discuss any of his encounters with the greatest boxers of all time, or the details of the fights that eventually led to his condition, he died of complications from pneumonia.

Beginning in the 1970s, as players in professional football and hockey began sustaining greater numbers of concussions and head injuries, doctors settled on something called "Quigley's rule" as the accepted method for avoiding long-lasting cognitive effects: a player should retire after sustaining three concussions. Within the past two years, however, this rule has been refined, as evidence shows that a greater amount of damage can occur after just two concussions, if they happen within a short period of time. Limiting the length of a career, if that career entails blows to the head, is no longer considered a guarantee of safety from brain damage.

A simple way to explain the mechanics of a concussion is to picture the brain as a yolk floating within a shell, or skull. If your bicycle hits a pothole and you're flying over the handlebars, or your jaw has just been hit by a fist traveling roughly thirty miles an hour, it's not the movement of your head but the sudden stop that causes the damage. Even if your head never hits the ground but rotates sideways, the velocity will cause the yolk that is your brain to crash against the inside your skull. This internal impact causes a large bruise, a subdural hematoma; small blood vessels in the brain break, and neurons, the nerve cells that transmit impulses to motor and speech skills, tear. The brain, like any other damaged body part, will swell. The clinical aftermath of this painful event is called "postconcussive syndrome," and to the layperson, it means any or all of a laundry list of symptoms, such as headaches, dizziness, memory loss, nausea, double vision, ringing in the ears, attention deficit, irritability, and general confusion, or what the medical profession calls "information-processing impairment." In order to determine the nature of the injury and the progress of the recovery from it, patients are asked to take a battery of tests of cognitive ability, memory, and other skills that could be irreparably damaged. Some brain functions never return to normal parameters, even in mild concussions.

For boxers, an added complication is when a hard punch lands in the face and snaps the head violently backward. This sort of straight-on blow causes the brain to rocket back against the skull, creating a coup lesion. The linear acceleration of the head jolting backward, with a sudden pinching back of the neck, causes an interruption of blood flow to the cerebellum: nerve damage at the base of the skull results. If this boxer is so stunned that he falls straight backward, hitting his head on the canvas, he creates another line of acceleration in the brain. The brain now sloshes rapidly forward, resulting in a contrecoup lesion: twice the damage for the price of a single concussion.

So far, studies show that somewhere between 9 and 25 percent of all professional boxers eventually suffer from boxing-induced dementia, as many as one in four. But a particularly brutal title fight is never examined, in the subsequent coverage, for its contribution to the dementia of the opponents after their retirement. The usual ravings are about how close each came to dying in the ring. For while most boxing fans would agree that a fight is more exciting if someone is suffering a cruel beating, the guilt of the spectators runs uncomfortably high when a boxer dies right

279

then and there: the complicity of the voyeur. As long as no one is dead afterward, a bloody bout is just a really good fight, the specter of future Jerry Quarrys notwithstanding.

Most of the recent deaths have occurred in the lower weight classes, such as 130-pound Jimmy Garcia, who was carried out of the ring on a stretcher during a fight in Las Vegas in 1995, only to die six days later, after an emergency operation to remove a blood clot from his brain. One theory as to why fighters in lower weight classes seem more susceptible to these fatal blood clots is that they may undertake drastic measures to make weight shortly before the bout, something heavyweight boxers need not worry about: a heavyweight can never be too heavy to fight. A boxer concerned about the weigh-in will abuse diuretics, exercise in steam rooms while wearing a rubber suit—anything that may help him drop as many as twenty pounds in as little as two days. These measures result in extreme dehydration, and the fluid lost can't be completely restored to the body in just one day before the fight. It's been suggested that the higher risk of death comes from the brain being surrounded by less fluid, and consequently less cushioning, making it more vulnerable in a concussion. Others believe that dehydration and the attendant electrolyte imbalances are the real danger. Improper levels of such minerals as potassium and sodium result in confusion, weakness, dizziness, and a loss of stamina, all things that would prevent a boxer from defending himself against lethal injury.

It's periodically suggested, usually after a widely publicized death, that headgear should be required of professional boxers. It's true that irreversible brain dysfunction is relatively rare among headgear-wearing amateur boxers, as various studies have shown, but the reasons may have little or nothing to do with the headgear itself. Amateurs fight in fewer bouts of shorter length, their careers span fewer years, and poor boxers will lose early and often and quit the sport, whereas the good ones will turn pro. Boxing headgear doesn't provide any protection against the velocity from a blow. A punch can cause whiplash, rotating the skull around at a speed that headgear can only exacerbate, increasing this pendulum effect. Headgear also absorbs sweat, which makes it weigh more, placing more strain upon the neck in a high-velocity situation, and it provides an opponent with a bigger, slower target to hit.

Deaths in the ring are well publicized, but surprisingly enough, they are extraordinarily rare, at only 0.13 per 1,000 participants. Sports with a far greater risk of death than boxing include parachuting, hang gliding, mountaineering, scuba diving, motorcycle racing, and even football. The sport with the highest reported rate of head injury is horseback riding: a staggering 91 percent of all riding accidents involve head trauma. (And yet my father, like countless others before and after him, encouraged me to "get back on the horse!" after a fall and was horrified when I began to box.)

If an ex-boxer does manage to escape the early onset of dementia, brain injuries are far from the only occupational hazard. The legendary cauliflower ear—so named because the ear can resemble the vegetable—comes from repeated blows to the ear and lack of medical care for the condition. A hard punch to the ear can rupture blood vessels under the skin, which then swell up in one spot. This hemorrhage will turn into a hardened, jellylike mass, and if it's not lanced, and if infection is not prevented or treated, the mass will eventually reabsorb on its own, but not without leaving fibrous scar tissue behind. Repeated injury to the same area exacerbates the problem; more and more fibrous tissue collects, and the delicate architecture of the ear is permanently distorted.

Renal masses have also been reported in ex-boxers, for while blows to the kidneys are illegal in boxing (as are punches below the belt), it doesn't mean they don't happen. Boxers have been diagnosed with fibrous cysts in the kidneys that were caused by hard blows in fights that took place perhaps twenty-five or even fifty years earlier.

But while renal masses are fairly rare, and cauliflower ears are more of a cosmetic issue, eye injuries are the real scourge of boxers and are common even among amateur boxers wearing headgear. The retina, the area inside the eye that is the projection screen for receiving images that are then transmitted to the optical nerve, is prone to detachment in boxers, but that's a dramatic event, obvious at the moment it happens. Any sharp blow to the eye, even from something like a tennis ball, can result in the retina becoming dislodged. When this happens, there is a sudden complete or partial loss of vision. In some cases, the appearance of numerous "floaters" indicates a serious problem, but without immediate medical attention after such an event, you could be blind within hours. When Sugar Ray Leonard retired from boxing after suffering a detached retina, emergency surgery saved his vision. One ex-boxer who teaches a no-sparring boxing class in a gym in Manhattan wasn't so lucky; he wears an eye patch over his blind eye.

In one 1993 study comparing 25 amateur boxers to 25 men in a control group who did not box (all of whom had 20/20 vision), 19 of the boxers were shown to have eye damage from "contusion trauma," that is, getting punched in the eye. Even though they showed no outward symptoms, retinal scars were seen in 15 of the boxers, and retinal tears and/or holes were seen in 6. Only one man in the control group had a retinal hole, and the rest had no abnormalities whatsoever.

Even today, when the overwhelming medical evidence is causing many to question the glorification of such a hazardous sport, and aspiring boxers themselves are aware of the dangers that come with a boxing career, many male boxers still feel that the risks are worth the potential for reward. For many of them, it's the career of last resort, the vocation of choice for the past hundred years for the lower socioeconomic classes. You don't see any male boxers who interrupted medical or law school in order to turn pro.

But as more and more women boxers enter the professional boxing ranks, their choice to box is never as a "way out of the ghetto," as it might be for a man, or as a viable option to make money out of brawn. The vast majority of female boxers, myself included, have the educational background to earn a living doing something else. For my part, my participation in the sport was enabled by what I can only term as my willing suspension of disbelief. As scared as I was at times, I never thought I'd die or end up severely, permanently disabled; my imagined worst-case scenarios involved a broken nose, broken ribs, black eyes. While I feared being knocked out, I believed, like Reggie Tuur, that it would take upward of fifty knockout punches to inflict real, lasting, Muhammad Ali–style damage.

The person who should be most aware of this kind of damage is Muhammad Ali's daughter Laila, who has launched a professional boxing career of her own. She has witnessed firsthand the heartbreaking physical decline of her father, which many attribute to his career, and still chooses to get in the ring; this, to me, seems suicidal. However, she's not alone. Joe Frazier's daughter Jacquelyn Frazier-Lyde has also—at the age of thirty-nine—turned pro and faced off against Laila Ali in a second-generation rematch of their fathers' famous rivalry. Fourteen thousand people turned out to see the fight.

The clamoring for female fighters began with the unexpected success and popularity of Christy Martin, the "coal miner's daughter" from West Virginia. Don King put her on with Dierdre Gogarty as the undercard to the Mike Tyson–Frank Bruno fight in March 1996. While Tyson easily knocked out a terrified Bruno in three rounds, it was Martin who stole the spotlight in a bloody, action-filled fight. Suddenly boxing was seen as a viable women's sport. Gyms nationwide, always looking for the next fitness craze, have been offering more boxing classes, and women have continued to sign up. According to *Time* magazine, the 400 female pros and more than 1,400 amateurs worldwide represent a fivefold increase over the numbers three years ago.

The main problem in promoting women's boxing has been finding female fighters with sufficient experience and technical skills to be something more than what an executive at HBO Sports has called "an organized catfight." Boxing promoters have therefore recruited the female progeny of legendary male fighters, knowing that their names will sell. The promise of a big paycheck has lured George Foreman's daughter Freeda, Archie Moore's daughter J'Marie, and Roberto Duran's daughter Irichelle. They have all recently declared themselves professional boxers. Not every father wants his daughter to follow in his footsteps, however. When Duran heard of Irichelle's plans, he didn't speak to her for a week. Joe Frazier offered his daughter $15,000 not to fight Laila Ali.

Just one year after I made the decision to stop boxing,

Katie Dallam of Jefferson City, Missouri, fought her first and last professional fight. A novice who was, like many women, largely untrained in defensive moves, she was matched against a woman of lighter weight but greater experience, and she was badly beaten. She nearly died afterward but recovered, although with permanent brain damage. Dallam, with a master's degree in social work, and an accomplished artist, can no longer live alone, drive, work, or paint. Her sister cares for her full time.

ACKNOWLEDGMENTS

My thanks to Pat Manocchia, my longtime friend and trainer, who showed me, against all previous evidence, that I am an athlete. Thank you for that continuing journey.

My deepest thanks and appreciation to Susan Kamil for her tireless dedication and quest for excellence, to Zoë Rice for her thoughtful attention to detail and inspired suggestions, and to Richard Pine for his unwavering belief, faith, and patience. Thanks also to Dr. Ziv Peled for his help in translating the medical texts into plain English, and to Dr. Richard Goldberg, who tended my injuries with such good humor. Thanks to my family for the unending support, love, and kindness during this difficult time, and also to my many friends at La Palestra. I treasure the many shared miles we've run.

Most of all, I thank my wonderful husband, Bronson Picket, whose love, support, enthusiasm, encouragement, strength, and willingness to listen, read, and talk about these experiences helped me find my voice to tell this story: my love, my thanks, my gratitude.

ABOUT THE AUTHOR

Lynn Snowden Picket's first book was *Nine Lives*. Her work appears regularly in *Mademoiselle* and *Gear*, and she has written for *George*, *Spin*, *Outside*, *Harper's Bazaar*, *Esquire*, and *The New York Times*. She lives with her husband in New York City.